THE NAZI FILES

THE NAZI FILES

CHILLING CASE STUDIES OF THE PERSONALITIES BEHIND THE THIRD REICH

Paul Roland

ARCTURUS

ARCTURUS

© 2015 Arcturus Holdings Limited

ISBN 978-1-78404-877-8
AD003900UK

Manufactured in Malaysia

2 4 6 8 10 9 7 5 3 1

Contents

Introduction

More than half a century after the Second World War the Nazis continue to exercise a morbid fascination, despite their abhorrent ideology and murderous deeds. But were they innately evil, or merely fatally flawed individuals corrupted by their messianic Führer, Adolf Hitler?

Evil is a theological concept which assumes that a malevolent force exists in the universe with the power to influence human affairs. But if this is a fallacy and we are all responsible for our own thoughts and actions, how do we explain the destructive impulse that impelled Hitler and his fanatical followers to order the cold-blooded murder of millions? And how can we understand the unquestioning obedience of those who implemented such orders with unbridled enthusiasm?

How could a devout Catholic such as Franz Stangl, commandant of Sobibor and Treblinka, send thousands of innocent men, women and children to the gas chambers? And how did Rudolf Hoess, commandant of Auschwitz, continue to live a normal family life with his children playing within sight and sound of the crematoria? Were the inhuman experiments conducted by Dr Josef Mengele in Auschwitz acts of pure sadism, or did he truly believe that his 'research' had scientific value? What possessed devoted mother Magda Goebbels to murder six of her children? And how did educated and cultured men such as Reinhard Heydrich and architect Albert Speer justify the brutal liquidation of the ghettos and the slave labour programme which saw thousands of men, women and children starved, beaten and worked to death for their 'superior' Aryan masters?

Such scenes might have been common in biblical times, but the barbarity meted out by the Nazis took place in the era of commercial air travel, wireless communication, cinema and the motor car. By the middle of the 20th century ignorance, superstition and blind obedience were assumed to have been a feature of the Dark Ages and yet Hitler and the Nazi leadership succeeded in seducing a nation that had produced some of the most significant philosophers, scientists and artists of the age, before leading the nation into a hell entirely of its own making.

PSYCHOLOGICAL TESTS

The first attempt to understand the minds of the Nazi leadership came in the immediate aftermath of the war in Europe, when 21 of Hitler's inner circle were incarcerated at Nuremberg awaiting trial for crimes against humanity. The Allied prosecution hoped that if some of the defendants were willing to submit to a series of psychological tests, they might learn what had made such apparently ordinary men commit such unspeakable crimes. With little to occupy them in the months leading up to the trial, Hermann Goering, Joachim von Ribbentrop, Rudolf Hess and Albert Speer agreed to take the tests under the supervision of two American experts – psychologist Gustave Gilbert, PhD and psychiatrist Douglas Kelley, MD.

Both Kelley and Gilbert concluded that all of the accused were legally sane, but they disagreed on their interpretation of the data. Gilbert declared that there were three distinct psychopathic types in the group, whom he categorized as schizoid, narcissistic and paranoid. He argued that they had been conditioned to defer to authority without question and so had not developed any critical faculties. In contrast, Kelley[1] contended that the defendants were the pathological product of a 'socio-cultural disease' and had been

---

[1] Ironically, Kelley committed suicide in 1958 using a cyanide capsule, just as Goering had done to cheat the hangman.

encouraged to commit criminal acts by their psychotic leader, like the brainwashed members of a religious cult. Once Hitler was gone, they reverted to their original unprepossessing personalities.

This well-intentioned attempt to understand the criminal mind was, however, fundamentally flawed. It was rather naïve to assume that a series of simple and highly subjective psychological tests could identify the various contributing factors that led to the development of such complex personality disorders and extreme aberrant behaviour.

LUST FOR POWER
Over the following pages I have attempted to profile 22 of the leading Nazis and their most devoted disciples in the hope of unearthing why their actions diverted

so drastically from acceptable human behaviour and how they justified their actions to themselves and their families. They all had their reasons, which suggests that evil cannot be conveniently categorized or accurately defined and that the Nazis were, on the whole, very common personality types who simply could not resist the primal urge to exercise unconstrained power over others.

They prove that there really is no such thing as the typical Nazi personality or mind-set. Anyone who relinquishes their integrity and compassion for their fellow human beings is capable of committing such unconscionable acts.

It was Hitler's distorted dream to bend the nation to his will, but what were his fellow Germans thinking when they obeyed him so slavishly?

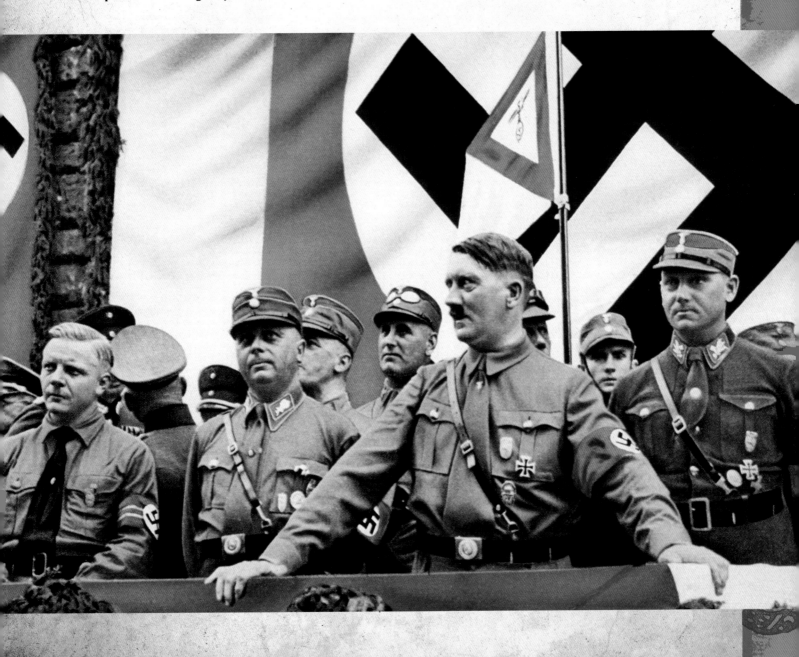

Martin Bormann

The Man They Loved to Hate

'In my dictionary DUTY is written in capitals.'

Martin Bormann was referred to contemptuously by his jealous rivals in the Nazi hierarchy as 'the brown eminence', an allusion to his shadowy presence and insidious influence over their leader. Goering, Goebbels, Himmler and the rest of the Hitler gang despised Bormann for the sycophantic fawning with which he had ingratiated himself with their beloved Führer, restricting their access to the leader, an act for which they never forgave him. In the words of an insider, Bormann 'erected a positive Chinese wall through which people were admitted only after showing their empty hands and explaining in detail to Bormann the purpose of their visit. By this means he had absolute control over the whole machinery of the Reich.'

Most Nazi bigwigs hated Bormann (eighth from right, turning away) because of the way he controlled access to Hitler (standing)

MARTIN BORMANN

BORN: 17 June, 1900, Wegeleben, Prussia
DIED: 2 May, 1945(?), West Berlin
NICKNAME: The Brown Eminence

Family: Born to Lutheran parents, Theodor and Antonie; one surviving sibling, Albert; two half-siblings, Else and Walter, from father's first marriage; wife, Gerda (died 1946); ten children, nine survived (Adolf Martin, Ilse, Irmgard, Rudolf, Heinrich, Eva, Gerda, Fred, Volker)

Career/life: Artillery soldier in final days of First World War; joined Freikorps; jailed for murder in 1924, with Rudolf Hoess; Reichstag member, 1933; secretary to Rudolf Hess, 1933–41; head of the Party Chancellery, 1941 and gained immense influence over Hitler; escaped from Führerbunker, 1945; tried and sentenced to death *in absentia* at Nuremberg; remains found in West Berlin, 1972, but authenticity disputed until DNA test in 1998

Description: Short and squat; fastidious attention to detail; brutal, coarse, lacking in culture, but skilled at political intrigue and manipulation; believed that Nazism and Christianity were incompatible; shared Hitler's hatred of Jews and Slavs; deliberately avoided public gaze

'Silence is usually the wisest course. And one should by no means always tell the truth...'

RIGHT-HAND MAN

A former personal secretary to Rudolf Hess, Bormann became the power behind the throne by making himself indispensable to Hitler and proving himself an able manager of the Führer's financial affairs. While the Nazi leaders flattered their Führer's ego by complimenting him on his strategic genius and his political shrewdness, Bormann worked quietly to increase Hitler's personal wealth and build his Alpine retreat, the Berghof at Berchtesgaden, in a style and manner befitting the father of the Third Reich. In the construction of the Berghof, Hitler's every whim had been indulged and no expense spared. Bormann also found favour by purchasing Hitler's birthplace at Braunau and his parents' house at Leonding and giving them as presents to Hitler. It was a shrewd and cynical move on Bormann's part, and one for which the inner circle resented him even more than they disliked and distrusted each other. Hans Frank, Governor-General of Poland, remarked that hatred was too weak a word to describe what the inner circle felt for Bormann, who always seemed to be hovering at Hitler's side in an ill-fitting suit, briefcase under his arm, poised to intercede on his leader's behalf if anyone spoke out of turn.

A short, squat figure with a moon face, he was described by those who knew him as 'coarse', 'banal' and 'a boot licker', but he was also dependable and uncommonly diligent. He didn't smoke or drink and ate sparingly in Hitler's presence, often sharing his Führer's preference for a vegetarian diet, but it was merely a ploy to appear modest and unpretentious. In secret, he gorged on pork chops and any other meat left over after the guests had gone.

It has been said that he didn't have an original idea in his head, that his wife Gerda was the ideologist in the family and that he simply repeated whatever she told him or overheard her saying in order to impress their guests. Observers reported that he was incapable of uttering a coherent sentence at a social gathering or of making small talk, and yet he would word his official communications and reports as succinctly as a clinician reporting on the result of an experiment.

IDEAL OFFICE MANAGER

His lack of imagination and personality made him the perfect assistant for a tyrant who tolerated no dissent and demanded blind obedience. In other words, he was a 'yes' man who would dutifully record his leader's every utterance and observation, no matter how banal,

as if it were the profound insights of an Einstein or an eminent philosopher.

Shortly after Bormann succeeded Rudolf Hess as Hitler's 'private secretary', Alfred Rosenberg noted,

'Hess had obviously got on the Führer's nerves, and so Bormann took care of the queries and orders. Here is where he began to make himself indispensable. If, during our dinner conversation, some incident was mentioned, Bormann would pull out his notebook and make an entry. Or else, if the Führer expressed displeasure over some remark, some measure, some film, Bormann would make a note. If something seemed unclear, Bormann would get up and leave the room, but return almost immediately after having given orders to his office staff to investigate forthwith, and to telephone, wire or teletype.'

Bormann's official title gave the impression that he had no authority, but he was by Hitler's side whenever the Führer launched into one of his hysterical tirades against those he suspected of betrayal and was always ready with the names of those who were to blame. His advancement to the inner sanctum of the Reich Chancellery baffled those who assumed Hitler would promote those who had demonstrated bravery in the field, but the 'Bohemian corporal', as the Führer was disparagingly known, was unimpressed by acts of self-sacrifice and courage, which he considered obligatory when under fire. Hitler, it seems, was more impressed by fastidious attention to detail, thoroughness, order and industry, the importance of which had been beaten into him by his father, a provincial customs officer: qualities which Bormann possessed and which made him the ideal office manager.

Hitler was recorded as saying,

THE BORMANN DOSSIER

> Bormann enlisted as an artillery man in the Second World War but he didn't see active service.

> His father had been a sergeant-major who was employed by the post office after he left the army.

> Bormann was one of the few Nazi leaders to have committed murder with his own hands. In 1924 he was sentenced to one year in prison for killing his former elementary school teacher, Walther Kadow, whom he suspected of informing on a Nazi saboteur. Bormann's co-defendant was the future commandant of Auschwitz, Rudolf Hoess.

> On 17 June 1941 Bormann issued a secret directive to all regional Gauleiters to destroy the power of the Church. He believed that Nazi ideology would not replace Christianity until the influence of the Church had been completely eradicated. 'National Socialist and Christian concepts are incompatible. The Christian churches build upon men's ignorance; by contrast, National Socialism rests upon scientific foundations... But never again must the churches be allowed any influence over the leadership of the people. This must be broken totally and forever.'

> He was instrumental in persuading Hitler to order the extermination of the Jews. On 19 August 1942 Bormann drafted a memo stating 'the permanent elimination of the Jews from the territories of Greater Germany can no longer be carried out by emigration but by the use of ruthless force in the special camps of the East'.

> In July 1943 Bormann suggested that Eichmann be given responsibility for organizing the transportation of the Jews to extermination camps. The other three candidates for the job were all doctors at Auschwitz.

> He kept a card index file on party members and officials whom he distrusted and another on those that he could coerce into serving as informers.

> His wife Gerda agreed to share her home with his mistress and encouraged him to father more children with the woman known only as 'M'. Gerda had given birth to ten children of her own, nine of whom had survived into childhood.

> After Hitler had ordered the arrest of Hermann Goering for attempting to negotiate a surrender with the Allies, Bormann altered it to a death warrant. But Goering surrendered before the SS could kill him.

> Bormann was the official witness to Hitler's marriage to Eva Braun in the Berlin bunker at midnight on 29 April 1945, the night before they killed themselves to avoid capture by the Russians.

'I know that Bormann is brutal. But there is sense in everything he does and I can absolutely rely on my orders being carried out by Bormann immediately and in spite of all obstacles. Bormann's proposals are so precisely worked out that I have only to say yes or no. With him I deal in ten minutes with a pile of documents for which with another man I should need hours. If I say to him, remind me about such and such a matter in half a year's time, I can be sure that he will really do so.'

QUIET RISE TO POWER

Bormann knew that real power and influence did not lie in titles and symbols but with having the ear and confidence of the leader. In this respect, he was the antithesis of Goering. While Goering strutted the world stage in gaudy uniforms and boasted of the titles bestowed upon him by an indulgent Führer, Bormann bided his time, manoeuvring himself into a position from where he was able to marginalize those officials he feared or distrusted and assimilate their responsibilities for himself.

Rosenberg, Ley and Reich Minister Lammers all found themselves excluded from the decision-making process and unable to bring their concerns to Hitler because they assumed, or were led to believe, that the Führer was displeased with them and they didn't dare risk incurring further displeasure by appealing to him to reconsider.

The loyal lieutenant's proximity to Hitler ensured that the Führer heard Bormann's version of events before any of the other leaders had their chance to present the facts and in this way Bormann shielded his leader from the harsh reality of imminent defeat during the final days in the Führer bunker. On one occasion Bormann returned a dossier of photographs sent by Goebbels, which depicted the destruction of German cities, with a desultory note to the effect that the Führer didn't want to be troubled with 'trivial matters'. And when Goebbels submitted a detailed assessment of the desperate military situation, Bormann filed it at the back of his safe where it lay unread until after Hitler's death.

But he was much more than a self-serving, ruthlessly ambitious assistant. As Hitler became increasingly incapacitated and delusional, Bormann interpreted Hitler's offhand remarks as edicts, initiating orders which led to the murder of hundreds of thousands of Slavs. Their lives were of no value, he declared. Their women should abort, the more the better, to speed the extinction of the race. They would be allowed to keep their religion because it served as a 'diversion', but their towns and villages were to be destroyed. They existed only to serve their German masters.

WHERE DID HE GO?

Ironically, for a man for whom anonymity was prized as much as influence, Bormann became better known after the war than he had been during his lifetime. During the Nazis' rise to power he was rarely seen in public and all through the war he deliberately kept a low profile. But after he had been condemned to death *in absentia* at the Nuremberg Trials, his part in the regime became common knowledge. The belated interest in Bormann was partly due to the fact that his fate was to remain a mystery for more than 50 years. Had he escaped along the 'rat line' to South America? Had he fallen into the hands of the advancing Russians when they stormed the Führerbunker? Or had he been killed in the breakout and buried in the rubble of Berlin? There were even rumours that Churchill had ordered him to be smuggled out of Germany so he could help the Allies recover Nazi gold from Swiss bank accounts.

The discovery of what were thought to be his remains in 1972, near the Lehrter railway station in Berlin, did not silence the speculation. It was only in 1998 that the corpse was positively identified as being that of Bormann, after it became possible to compare its DNA with that of one of his surviving family members.

A bemedalled Martin Bormann, sitting next to Goebbels, Hitler and Hess in a German beer keller, is the only one smiling

Adolf Hitler

Profiling the Great Dictator

'A survey of the raw material, in conjunction with our knowledge of Hitler's actions as reported in the news, was sufficient to convince us that he was, in all probability, a neurotic psychopath.'

Walter C. Langer

Psychological profiling is commonly used by law enforcement agencies in almost every country in the world to provide a description of the Unsub (the Unknown Subject) – their personality type, marital status, age, occupation, etc. – when there is a lack of physical evidence and there are no eyewitnesses. One of the earliest applications of this technique was the profile of Adolf Hitler compiled in 1943 by American psychoanalyst Walter C. Langer for the United States Office of Strategic Services (OSS), which later became the CIA.

Langer's superiors hoped that after interviewing dozens of German exiles who were known to have had direct contact with the dictator, and by sifting through thousands of reports from intelligence sources, Langer might uncover some damaging facts that could be used for propaganda purposes. But they also needed to know how susceptible Hitler might be to their deception tactics, designed to divert his forces from potential Allied landing sites, and how he might react if the war went against him.

CHARISMA RIDDLE

Allied propaganda portrayed the German dictator as an unpredictable hysteric, susceptible to violent mood swings, but such a simplified image did not explain the adoration lavished upon him by the vast majority of Germans and by Nazi sympathizers abroad. German newsreels depicted Hitler as a charismatic saviour, the man who had mesmerized a nation, revitalized its economy and restored its pride after the humiliating

defeat of 1918. Foreign politicians and diplomats, together with celebrities such as the American aviator Charles Lindbergh, had praised Hitler during highly publicized visits to Germany in the early 1930s. Several impressionable members of the British aristocracy including the Mitford sisters, Diana and Unity, and the future Duke and Duchess of Windsor, had fawned at his feet to the embarrassment of the British government. Even the young John Kennedy, future president of the United States, had written of his admiration for Hitler's economic 'miracle'. There were many in Europe and America who regarded Hitler as the kind of strong and decisive leader that was needed to haul their nation out of the Great Depression and stem the spread of communism which threatened democracy.

How could Langer account for Hitler's charismatic hold over so many supposedly intelligent, well-educated people and their governments' apparent willingness to appease him and acquiesce to his demands?

In his opening remarks, Langer acknowledged that it might be convenient to see one's enemy as 'evil' incarnate and to believe that eliminating a tyrant will restore order, but such a simple view does not address the extraordinary conditions that produced such a man, nor acknowledge the national neurosis that brought him to power. As he observed,

Some people are happy with candles and a cake, but for Hitler's 50th birthday on 20 April 1939 there was a huge parade in Berlin

ADOLF HITLER

BORN: 20 April, 1889, Braunau am Inn, Austria-Hungary
DIED: 30 April, 1945, Berlin, Germany
NICKNAME: Wolf, Alf, the Bohemian corporal

Family: Father: Alois Hitler (formerly Schicklgruber); mother: Klara Hitler (née Pölzl); sibling: Paula (Gustav, Ida, Edmund and Otto had died in childhood); half-siblings: Alois, Angela; wife: Eva (née Braun)

Career/life: Mediocre school record; bohemian life in Vienna, 1905–13; moved to Munich, 1913; corporal in Bavarian Army in First World War, wounded and decorated; joined German Workers' Party in 1919, which changed its name to NSDAP – Hitler became leader in 1921; jailed after failed Munich Putsch, 1923, dictated most of first volume of *Mein Kampf* while in prison, which was published 1925/26 and became great success; connected to suicide of niece, Geli Raubal in 1931; became German Chancellor, 1933; Enabling Bill, 1933, gave him dictatorial powers; purged SA, 1934, leaving SS dominant; accelerated Jewish persecution with Nuremberg Laws, 1935, which took away Jewish citizenship; rearmed Germany and invaded Rhineland, 1936; made Austria part of Germany, 1938; acquired Sudetenland for Germany, 1938; invaded Poland in 1939, which was followed by British and French declarations of war, beginning the Second World War; Germany's defeat in Second World War led to suicide in 1945

Description: Sexually shy in younger days and unusually close to mother; no apparent sex life as adult, yet attractive to women; displayed feminine characteristics, some thought; suffered from a number of physical ailments; infantile tastes, such as eating large numbers of cream cakes; unprepossessing general appearance, but piercing gaze; ability to hypnotize audiences; rabid anti-Semite; flew into rages when challenged; given to monologues; messiah-like tendencies, feeling of omnipotence, but also appeared insecure

'Struggle is the father of all things, virtue lies in blood, leadership is primary and decisive.'

'It was not only Hitler, the madman, who created German madness, but German madness which created Hitler. Having created him as its spokesman and leader, it has been carried along by his momentum... it continues to follow his lead in spite of the fact that it must be obvious to all intelligent people now that his path leads to inevitable destruction.'

FALSE MESSIAH

Hitler believed that his destiny and that of Germany were mutually dependent and he convinced the German people that their fate would be determined by their loyalty to him, the father of the nation. But their saviour was to prove a false messiah. In Langer's opinion, and that of the three independent psychoanalysts who verified his findings, Hitler was a malignant narcissist and prey to a multiplicity of neuroses which only became apparent when his delusions of grandeur were shattered in the last months of the war.

As the Allies encircled Berlin he would blame Germany's imminent defeat on the nation's lack of moral courage and punish its citizens for their betrayal by ordering the destruction of the country's infrastructure, thereby depriving them of the means of recovering after he had deserted them.

'The world has come to know Adolf Hitler for his insatiable greed for power, his ruthlessness, cruelty and utter lack of feeling, his contempt for established institutions and his lack of moral restraints,' wrote Langer, '... he initiated the most brutal and devastating war in history – a war which, for a time, threatened the complete destruction of our civilization. Human life and human suffering seem to leave this individual completely untouched as he plunges along the course he believes he was predestined to take... The problem of our study should be, then, not only whether Hitler is mad or not, but what influences in his development have made him what he is.'

Hitler in Nuremberg in the early 1930s with his fellow Brownshirts – his Mercedes Benz was armoured in case of assassination attempts

BAD BLOOD OR BAD SEED?

> *'These people [journalists] must never find out who I am. They mustn't know where I come from or my family background.'*
>
> Hitler, quoted in Hitler: A Biography, *Joachim Fest, 1973*

Hitler's family tree produced only one bad apple, but more than its share of damaged fruit. Family physician Dr Bloch claimed that mental disorders and physical disability were prevalent in the paternal branch, whose itinerant farm labourer members had been intermarrying for generations; a fact which would account for Hitler's fear of inherent insanity and might explain why he refused to have children.

Hitler's younger sister and only surviving sibling, Paula, was mentally retarded, his aunt Johanna was a schizophrenic and his cousin Eduard Schmidt was born a hunchback with a severe speech impediment. Josef Veit, a cousin of Hitler's father, fathered three mentally retarded children, one of whom committed suicide after being confined to an asylum. But potentially more embarrassing for the future Führer was the criminal record of Hitler's half-brother Alois Matzelsberger (who later adopted the surname Hitler). Alois was

A rare picture of the young Hitler, aged ten, at school in Lambach; he was by no means an outstanding pupil

BAD SEED

> Hitler was a sickly child whose mother had suffered several miscarriages which led her to become overly protective. Her indulgence led to his 'over-identification' with her, which 'severely compromised his masculinity' and might have led to Hitler becoming a 'passive homosexual'.

> Henry Murray, a prominent American psychologist who lectured at Harvard University for 30 years, analyzed the metaphors in *Mein Kampf* and concluded that Hitler was both impotent and a 'fully fledged masochist'. Murray theorized that Hitler was driven to over-compensate for his sexual inadequacy through aggression, while author Lothar Machtan argued in his book *The Hidden Hitler* that the dictator was homosexual.

> Hitler hated his younger brother, seeing him as a rival for his mother's attention, and fantasized about killing him. The boy subsequently died.

> Hitler hated his father, Alois, a sadistic overbearing bully who beat his children, and prayed for the old man's death. Alois too died soon after.

ROOTS AND RUMOURS

It was rumoured that Hitler's paternal grandfather might have been a Jew from Graz called Frankenberger, who seduced his paternal grandmother Maria Anna Schicklgruber while she was employed as a maid in his household.

That is why he ordered his grandmother's tombstone to be removed, and all trace of her grave destroyed after he came to power. Even the parish records were burnt on Hitler's orders, to erase all documented proof of his father Alois's birth.

If there was no truth in the rumour, why did Hitler order four separate investigations into his ancestry between 1932 and 1940 and why did he have his father's birthplace of Döllersheim levelled to the ground?

It has also been claimed that Hitler subjected himself to periodic bleeding to 'purge' himself of his 'contaminated' Jewish blood.

One symptom of Hitler's neurosis was 'transference', in which subjects unconsciously offload their internal conflicts on to other individuals. This tendency to blame others for one's personal failings is typical of neurotic paranoid personalities. As Langer noted, 'By this process the Jew became a symbol of everything which Hitler hated in himself.'

twice convicted of theft and had been jailed for bigamy. After deserting his family he worked in a beer keller in Berlin and agreed to keep a low profile and not talk to the newspapers, though what price, if any, Hitler paid for his co-operation is not known – unless the threat of a visit from the Gestapo was enough to silence him. Himmler ensured that these potentially embarrassing facts were kept secret and it was only after the war that they were discovered in Gestapo files.

But there were also contributing factors closer to home.

Hitler's mother and father were second cousins and had married when she became pregnant. He was 46 and she was just 22. Klara and Alois had been intimate while he was still married to his second wife, Franziska, who was then dying of tuberculosis. Her death left Klara wracked by guilt and when their first two children died in infancy, followed by a third at the age of six, Klara, a strict Catholic, saw it as divine punishment for having deceived Franziska. Her constant fretting over the health of her children and her fastidious cleaning of their home left her only surviving son with a neurotic fear of germs and an obsession with death.

PERSONALITY DISORDER

The combination of his mother's over-indulgence and his father's brutal beatings and continual criticism instilled a toxic mixture of repressed anxiety and anger in the boy. One of Hitler's teachers recognized the flaws in his former pupil when he gave an assessment of Hitler at his trial following the Munich Putsch in 1924.

Professor Huemer testified that Hitler was 'gifted' in certain subjects but described him as lacking in self-control.

'To say the least, he was considered argumentative, autocratic, self-opinionated and bad-tempered and unable to submit to school discipline. Nor was he industrious, otherwise he would have achieved much better results, gifted as he was.'

More revealing is Hitler's assessment of his teachers, whom he described as 'erudite apes', 'abnormal', 'effete' and 'mentally deranged', adjectives which betray his own inferiority complex. His belligerence and barely suppressed hostility endeared him to few of his classmates.

The closest the adolescent Adolf came to having a friend was August Kubizek, who remembered,

'He saw everywhere only obstacles and hostility. He was always up against something and at odds with the world... I never saw him take anything lightly.'

FEAR OF INTIMACY

A rough sketch drawn by a classmate shows the 15-year-old Adolf as an unprepossessing youth, but not a boy the local girls would have avoided on looks alone. The fact that Hitler shunned close relationships of any kind suggests something more than adolescent self-consciousness.

A fear of intimacy which leads to obsessive fantasizing about the opposite sex and the belief that one is involved in a romantic relationship which does not exist is known as erotomania. Hitler exhibited such symptoms in his imagined romance with a young Jewish girl called Stefanie Rabatsch, while he and Kubizek were living in Vienna. Hitler wrote to her but couldn't muster the courage to talk to her, although he spoke to his friend incessantly of his plans to meet and marry her once he had made a name for himself. It wouldn't be unreasonable to assume that his frustrated 'romance' fed his later anti-Semitism.

It is surely significant that thereafter Hitler rejected the idea of adhering to a conventional moral code, or of acting according to his conscience. Conscience, he declared, was a Jewish concept and therefore it was every German's duty to distrust it and free themselves of the 'dirty and degrading [idea of] conscience and morality'.

TEATIME WITH HITLER

If any of the numerous foreign dignitaries and visitors to the Berghof, Hitler's Bavarian mountain retreat, hoped to glimpse Germany's leader in the throes of inspiration, possessed by the spirit that had made him such a powerful public speaker and enthralling his guests with penetrating insights on the current situation, they were likely to be gravely disappointed.

In private, the dictator reverted to the habits of his indolent youth, lying in bed until midday and staying up late to watch mawkishly sentimental movies that only Eva Braun could have found entertaining. When he finally emerged he would lounge in his favourite armchair in *bürgerlich* (petit bourgeois) fashion and indulge in long monologues on his pet subjects, which his inner circle had heard so often that they could recite whole passages by heart. But at least they knew when to laugh and when their host expected an encouraging nod or grunt of agreement.

Hitler built a fantasy home, the Berghof, in the Bavarian mountains. He might have been a riveting presence in front of a crowd, but the private man proved to be a cold fish in his own private domain

TRIVIAL PURSUITS

Hitler was a creature of habit. His press chief observed, 'He remained perpetually in the same company, among the same faces in the same atmosphere and, I may also say, in the same state of monotony and boredom, producing eternally the same speeches and declarations.'

Topics included his favourite film actresses, the early years of the Party, his personal sacrifices to ensure its success and the scandalous indiscretions of high-ranking Party members – which would be heard with feigned astonishment by guests who tried hard not to betray the fact that they had heard it all before.

A foreign office official observed, 'Concerning people, Hitler's judgements were usually bitter and derogatory. Qualities such as forbearance, humour and self-irony were completely foreign to him.'

The only time he was seen to laugh was at the expense of others (a German trait known as *Schadenfreude* or taking pleasure from another's misfortunes). According to his architect and armaments minister Albert Speer, 'He seemed to enjoy destroying the reputation and self-respect of even his close associates and faithful comrades.'

Hitler with his beloved Blondi, a gift from Martin Bormann: he called one of her puppies Wolf after himself. Adolf means 'noble wolf'.

On those rare occasions when Hitler talked of his childhood he criticized his father for being an alcoholic and spoke admiringly of his mother, but Langer concluded, 'No person manifesting Hitler's pathological personality traits could possibly have grown up in the idyllic home environment Hitler himself has described.'

Speer was also disappointed by the level of conversation and the time Hitler wasted on gossip and trivialities.

> '*The repertory remained the same. He neither extended nor deepened it, scarcely ever enriched it by new approaches. He did not even try to cover up the frequent repetitions. I cannot say I found his remarks very impressive.*'

Hitler was an avowed vegetarian who took a perverse delight in telling his meat-eating guests that their steaks looked like a dead baby and occasionally describing the process by which the animal had met its fate on the farm or in the slaughterhouse.

It is said that he amused himself by telling female guests that their make-up had been manufactured from human fat, but as he was known to abhor women who wore a lot of cosmetics it might be that he actually believed this old wives' tale.

UNSOPHISTICATED TASTES

But if their host was not the most stimulating company, at least there were always copious quantities of fresh cream cakes and chocolates to go round. Hitler had a sweet tooth and a simple if unsophisticated taste in just about everything else. His reading was said to be confined to the sentimental historical adventures of Karl May (author of the Native American 'Winnetou' series), his preference for architecture favoured the bombastic and his taste in art celebrated adolescent heroic fantasies of conflict, motherhood and sacrifice. Only his religious devotion to the music of Richard Wagner offered a release from the demons that tormented him. As his school friend August Kubizek observed, 'Wagner's music produced in him that escape into a mystical dream world which he needed in order to endure the tensions of his turbulent nature.'

Those who were privy to his meetings with Nazi

Hitler visits the Haus der Deutschen Kunst, Munich in 1939, where only 'approved art' was on show. Bormann lurks in the background

officials were astonished to see how quickly and casually he decided important matters of state. He didn't attempt to disguise his impatience with people he considered his inferiors or with matters that didn't interest him. And he deliberately surrounded himself with sycophants who would endorse his self-image of infallibility. As his press secretary remarked,

'Instead of drawing to himself men of high character, rich experience and breadth of vision, he gave such persons a wide berth and made sure they had no chance to influence him...[He] permitted no other gods beside himself.'

Hitler's Women

UNITY MITFORD
Hitler's Aristocratic Stalker

'A Perfect Example of Aryan Womanhood...'

Adolf Hitler

Women were often powerless to resist the fatal attraction of Adolf Hitler. Three are known to have committed suicide, including his 23-year-old niece, and rumours surrounding his strange relationship with several others raise intriguing questions regarding the dictator's ambivalent attitude towards the opposite sex.

POWER OVER WOMEN

Hitler was worshipped by millions of women. It all began as early as his trial following the Munich Putsch, when the courtroom was crammed with female admirers. Later on, almost half of the audiences that gathered to hear him speak were women. In newsreels they can be seen fainting, screaming, crying with emotion at the sight of him. Yet it was not only German women who found him so attractive – he also had ardent admirers among the British aristocracy, the most notorious being sisters Diana and Unity Mitford, daughters of the 2nd Baron Redesdale, a wealthy landowner from an ancient family.

Some members of the British aristocracy, including Lord Redesdale, felt threatened in the 1930s, fearing that their increasingly tenuous claim to power and wealth could be eroded by a communist takeover, aided by a Jewish world conspiracy – not to mention the trade unions. The man who was capable of dealing with all three threats, they thought, was Adolf Hitler. Even better, he actually seemed to admire the English nobility.

In the 1930s and 1940s, Hitler received the kind of attention from women that is reserved for pop singers and films stars today

EARLY FASCIST LEANINGS

As a teenager Unity decorated her bedroom wall with newspaper cuttings and swastikas. It was her way of getting her father's approval and attention from her five sisters, whom she thought prettier and more accomplished than she was. She later attended communist meetings dressed in the black shirt of the British Union of Fascists, gave the Hitler salute and heckled the speakers, to the annoyance of the fascist leader Oswald Mosley. Mosley married her sister Diana

Unity Mitford completely worshipped Hitler. In turn, he described her as 'a perfect specimen of Aryan womanhood'

in a private civil ceremony in Berlin at Goebbels' home in 1936 (reputedly with Hitler as the sole witness).

Three years earlier Unity and Diana had travelled to Germany to attend the Nuremberg Party rally as official BUF delegates and it was there that Unity's adolescent infatuation intensified into obsession. She determined to return and meet Hitler in person, frequenting the Munich café where he was known to hold court and take afternoon tea, waiting patiently every day for months on end for him to acknowledge her.

MEETING THE FÜHRER

Hitler finally invited her to his table. 'It was the most wonderful and beautiful [day] of my life,' she told her father. 'I am so happy that I wouldn't mind a bit, dying. I'd suppose I am the luckiest girl in the world. For me he is the greatest man of all time.'

It is unlikely he was attracted by her beauty, for there is no evidence that he engaged in a normal sexual relationship with any woman and every indication that he avoided intimacy at all costs. Nor was he influenced by her curious choice of middle name, 'Valkyrie', bestowed on her by her father, Lord Redesdale, who Mosley had described as 'one of nature's fascists'. It is more likely that her girlish admiration fed Hitler's narcissism and that he was intrigued to learn that her grandfather had translated his favourite book, Houston Stewart Chamberlain's racist diatribe *The Foundations of the Nineteenth Century*, and been a friend of his favourite composer, Richard Wagner.

Unity referred to Hitler in her letters home as 'Wolf' and wouldn't believe a word said against him. Shortly after he had given orders for the massacre of SA leader Ernst Roehm and hundreds of former associates in the 'Night of the Long Knives' Unity wrote, 'Poor sweet Führer, he's having such a *dreadful* time.'

At first Hitler appeared polite but distant and it was only when Goering mentioned that the Führer disliked women wearing make-up that she toned it down and found herself more in favour. But she was evidently regarded as an oddball by others in the Nazi hierarchy. Some found her relentless heel-clicking and saluting laughable.

Not having a romantic interest in the besotted British socialite, Hitler would have been unaware of the effect her presence was having on his live-in mistress Eva Braun, who confided to her diary, 'She is known as the Valkyrie and looks the part, including her legs. I, the mistress of the greatest man in Germany and the whole world, I sit here waiting while the sun mocks me through the window panes.' But Braun knew how to win her man back. She attempted suicide in May 1935 by swallowing an overdose of sleeping pills, an act which appealed to Hitler's sense of melodrama. Duly impressed, he distanced himself from Unity and devoted himself to Braun, allowing her to stay overnight at his Munich apartment.

Unity still persisted, unwilling to be deprived of the man she had set her heart on, but her feelings were not reciprocated.

MORE NAZI THAN THE NAZIS

Her passion for fascism, however, remained undiminished and she spoke at various rallies and wrote anti-Semitic editorials for *Der Stürmer*, which drew condemnation from the British press.

> 'The English have no notion of the Jewish danger. Our worst Jews work only behind the scenes. We think with joy of the day when we will be able to say England for the English! Out with the Jews! Heil Hitler! P.S. please publish my name in full, I want everyone to know I am a Jew hater.'

Hitler rewarded her with a gold Party badge and a private box at the 1936 Olympic Games. But back home, British Intelligence had opened a dossier on the woman described as being 'more Nazi than the Nazis' and it was getting fatter by the day. Guy Lidell, head of MI5, summed up her activities in his diary, which remained classified until 2002.

> 'Unity Mitford had been in close and intimate contact with the Führer and his supporters for several years, and was an ardent and open supporter of the Nazi regime. She had remained behind after the outbreak of war and her action had come perilously close to high treason.'

UNITY MITFORD

BORN: 8 August, 1914, London, England
DIED: 28 May, 1948, Oban, Scotland
NICKNAME: The Valkyrie, Boud

Family: Father: Lord Redesdale; mother: Sydney (née Gibson-Bowles); siblings: Jessica, Diana, Nancy, Deborah, Pamela, Thomas

Life: Joined British Union of Fascists, 1932; travelled in fascist delegation to Germany, 1933, heard Hitler speak and was smitten; returned in 1934, and finally met Hitler and became close to him; engaged in anti-Semitic activities, to Hitler's approval; stayed alongside Hitler for five years; shot herself in suicide attempt when war was declared (though conspiracy theories abound) and brought back to Britain in 1940, where she died eight years later

Description: Very tall, plain-looking with a large head, perhaps felt overwhelmed by her pretty and accomplished sisters

On the day that war was declared between Britain and Germany, she shot herself in the head with a pearl-handled pistol Hitler had given her.

Incredibly, she survived and was brought back to Britain, where she eventually died eight years later from an infection of the brain as a result of her self-inflicted wound.

Eva Braun now had the Führer's undivided attention.

HITLER'S BABY?

In 2002 declassified documents cast doubt on the 'myth' of Unity's attempted suicide. MI5 chief Guy Lidell had written at the time, 'We had no evidence to support the press allegations that she was in a serious state of health and it might well be that she was brought in on a stretcher in order to avoid publicity and unpleasantness to her family.'

Observer journalist Martin Bright claimed to have discovered a sealed file in the National Archives detailing a romantic liaison between Unity and a married RAF officer – a relationship that would appear inconsistent with her injuries.

Rather more fanciful is the claim that Unity gave birth to a baby in 1940 and that the alleged birth was covered up with the knowledge of the British authorities. The claim was made by a relative of a woman who ran the private maternity hospital that cared for Unity after her return to England. If she was indeed recovering from a head wound or a nervous breakdown a maternity hospital would seem an odd choice of place for her to convalesce.

But the rumour is unfounded according to Elmar Streicher, son of the infamous Julius Streicher. 'She had nothing to do with Hitler as a woman, she was just a butterfly to a flower. As a woman she was so very tall, you had to laugh to see it. She simply wasn't sexy. She was a virgin to the day of her death, I'd put my hand in the fire to say that.'

However other members of Hitler's inner circle talked of her affairs with SS officers, so if there is any truth in the rumour of her being pregnant on her return to England in 1940 it could have been by someone other than Hitler. But no record of the birth was filed at the maternity hospital and no mention of it was made in the numerous letters written between the sisters.

When she was reunited with her family Unity confessed, 'I thought you all hated me but I don't remember why.'

EARLY EXPERIENCES WITH WOMEN

According to an adolescent acquaintance, Reinhold Hanisch, Hitler's first love was the sister of his only close friend, August Kubizek.

Kubizek recalled Hitler being infatuated with a young Jewish girl called Stefanie Rabatsch while living in Vienna. He wrote her a long emotive poem 'Hymn to the Beloved', but never had the courage to speak to her.

It was rumoured that Hitler and Kubizek had frequented Vienna's red light district to observe the prostitutes that both fascinated and repulsed the young Hitler and that he had caught syphilis from a Jewish prostitute, but the rumours were never substantiated.

Hanisch remembers,

> 'Hitler had very little respect for the female sex, but very austere ideas about relations between men and women... He used to lecture us about this, saying every woman can be had... He often said that it was the woman's fault if a man went astray. A decent man can never improve a bad woman, but a woman can improve a man.'

While on holiday from high school Hitler met a milkmaid who tried to seduce him, but he ran away and bragged to his friends that this demonstrated his great self-control. It is Hanisch's opinion, however, that Hitler fled because he feared 'the eventual consequences'. Hanisch believed that in Vienna Hitler was so poor and so malnourished that it prevented him from having anything to do with women. 'Besides, his queer idealism about love would have kept him from any frivolous adventures.'

Hitler attracted many matronly admirers who sought to mother him while he was struggling to establish himself as a radical politician in Munich during the Depression.

Carola Hoffman, Victoria von Dirksen and Helena Bechstein, wife of the piano manufacturer, were three early devotees. Helena was distraught when he was sentenced to a year in prison after the failed putsch, but would not be put off. She posed as his mother in order to visit him, but her ardour cooled after he refused to marry her daughter Lottie. Hitler gifted the girl one of his watercolours with a personal dedication, 'To my beloved Lottie, your Wolf', but her mother was not placated and became a severe critic after the courtship had cooled. She may also have turned against him because she discovered she had a rival, one who was also ready to play the part of Germany's First Lady – Winifred Wagner, the wife of Siegfried, the composer's son. Siegfried was not a ladies' man to borrow the term of the time, which left his British-born wife unfulfilled and looking for romance elsewhere. She turned to the rising star of the far right and was soon singing his praises to all who would listen. 'This man is going to be the saviour of Germany,' she told them. How wrong can you be? By 1930 she was a widow and looking to hook husband number two, but Adolf was having none of it. They remained, however, 'good friends'.

Hitler chats with Winifred Wagner and her son Wieland at Villa Wahnfried, Bayreuth. Wieland called him 'Uncle Wolf'

ANGELA (GELI) RAUBAL
Fatal Attraction

'Geli was allowed to laugh at her Uncle Alf and adjust his tie when it had slipped.'

Baldur von Schirach

itler's one great love appears to have been his niece Geli Raubal, who allegedly committed suicide either because her uncle made 'unnatural demands' upon her, as some historians have claimed, or because he was insanely jealous of her younger admirers and she saw no chance of happiness. Hitler's official photographer, Heinrich Hoffmann, believed that her death embittered him to the extent that from that day on he could never again feel affection for any human being.

Geli was the youngest daughter of Hitler's half-sister Angela and lived with her mother and 'Uncle' Adolf in Haus Wachenfeld on the Obersalzberg near Berchtesgaden (which Hitler later refurbished and renamed the Berghof). They came to Wachenfeld after Hitler's release from Landsdorf, where he had been imprisoned for instigating the failed Munich Putsch. Angela had offered to act as housekeeper and she believed that Geli would benefit from the bracing Alpine air and the company of a man who was expected to lead his party to victory in the regional elections.

KEPT PRISONER

At first, Angela was pleased that the pair were getting along so well, enjoying long walks in the mountains and sharing intimate conversations, but then she overheard visitors complaining that their leader was spending more time with her daughter than with his advisers. And soon after the rows began, all stemming from Adolf's refusal to allow Geli to live in Vienna and pursue a singing career.

Heinrich Hoffmann observed, 'He watched and gloated over her like some servant with a rare and lovely bloom, and to cherish and protect her was his one and only concern.' But it would seem that his attentions were not welcome and his demands were driving her towards a nervous breakdown. Hitler's former friend Ernst Hanfstaengl may have been closer to the truth about their relationship when he blamed Geli's death on Hitler's 'twisted tenderness'.

Geli complained to her mother that she was under constant surveillance whenever her uncle was away and was shadowed by his bodyguards on those rare occasions when he permitted her to visit the nearest town. His constant need to control her was suffocating and his insistence on choosing her clothes and the company she kept made her feel like a prisoner.

STRANGE DESIRES

But there may have been something more sinister behind Geli's decision to take her own life. According to Hitler biographer Konrad Heiden, a compromising letter written by Hitler to his niece fell into the hands of a potential blackmailer and had to be retrieved by a trusted priest, Father Staempfle. The contents of the letter were said to be so potentially damaging to Hitler's political career that the priest paid with his life on the Night of the Long Knives, in order to ensure his silence.

Heiden is of the opinion that the letter contained Hitler's admission that he needed Geli to satisfy his masochistic desires, for which there is no corroboration. However, according to a book by Otto Strasser, there were rumours at the time that there was 'something very unusual' about their relationship and that Hitler's demands proved 'unbearable' for her. She spoke of being desperately unhappy because she could not do 'what he wants me to'.

WAS IT SUICIDE?

Otto Strasser isn't the most reliable or unbiased source and there may have been a more innocent interpretation of the latter quote, namely that Hitler had forbidden Geli to leave for Vienna to study singing, or to see his young driver whom she was keen on. But whatever the truth, it is a fact that Geli was found dead from a single gunshot to the heart on the afternoon of 17 September 1931. Hitler's Walther pistol lay by the body and an unfinished note addressed to a friend was found nearby. It ended, 'When I come to Vienna – hopefully very soon – we'll drive together to Semmering

Adolf Hitler with Geli on a boat trip. Some people claim that she used to model naked so he could sketch her

ANGELA (GELI) RAUBAL

BORN: 4 June, 1908, Linz, Austria
DIED: 18 September, 1931, Munich, Bavaria
NICKNAME: Geli

Family: Father: Leo Raubal (died when she was two); mother: Angela (née Hitler); siblings: Leo, Elfriede

Life: Mother became Hitler's housekeeper when Geli was 17; moved into Hitler's Munich apartment, 1929, where she was almost a prisoner; after being forbidden to go to Vienna in 1931, she apparently committed suicide, shooting herself

Description: Looked more like a child than a grown-up girl, it was said. Not exactly pretty, but she had great natural charm. She usually went without a hat and wore very plain clothes, pleated skirts and white blouses. No jewellery except a gold swastika given to her by Uncle Adolf, whom she called Uncle Alf

'I love Geli and could marry her. Good! But you know what my viewpoint is. I want to remain single. So I retain the right to exert an influence on her circle of friends until such a time as she finds the right man.' Adolf Hitler

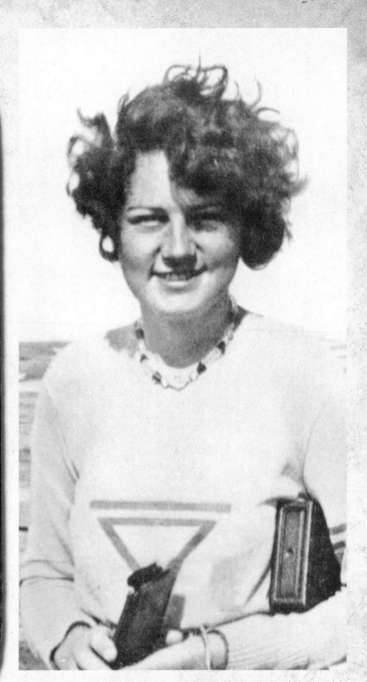

Geli Raubal: was Hitler merely keeping an avuncular eye on how she behaved or did he harbour unhealthy feelings towards her?

an...' It suggests that either she had broken off to plead with her uncle one last time as he left for Nuremberg (she had been heard to call out to him from an upstairs window, 'So you won't allow me to go to Vienna?', to which he curtly replied, 'No!') or she had been murdered to avoid a scandal that would certainly have ended his political career. But if she had been silenced, then it made no sense to leave the unfinished note – unless its significance hadn't occurred to whoever had pulled the trigger.

Her death is said to have left Hitler utterly inconsolable for a week during which time he barely left his room or communicated with anyone else, after which he ordered that her room be preserved as a shrine and her name never again be mentioned in his presence.

Sometime later he commissioned a portrait of his niece which he kept in his bedroom, together with a picture of his mother – the only two women he had ever really loved.

Eva Braun

Hitler's Devoted and Undemanding Companion

'Better that ten thousand others die than he be lost to Germany.'

Hitler respected only two types of women – the heroine and the matriarch. He admired mountaineer and film-maker Leni Riefenstahl for her passionate devotion to her art and for the physical endurance she exhibited in her early 'mountain films' and he held aviator Hanna Reitsch in the highest regard for offering to fly him out of Berlin in the final days. But he was said to be intimidated by such strong, assertive and independent women if they hinted at anything other than mutual admiration and reportedly rejected Riefenstahl's advances for that reason, although she claimed that she had spurned him because she didn't find him attractive.

Eva Braun (second left) at her parents' home in Munich in 1938, with her mother (centre) and her sisters, Ilse and Margarete

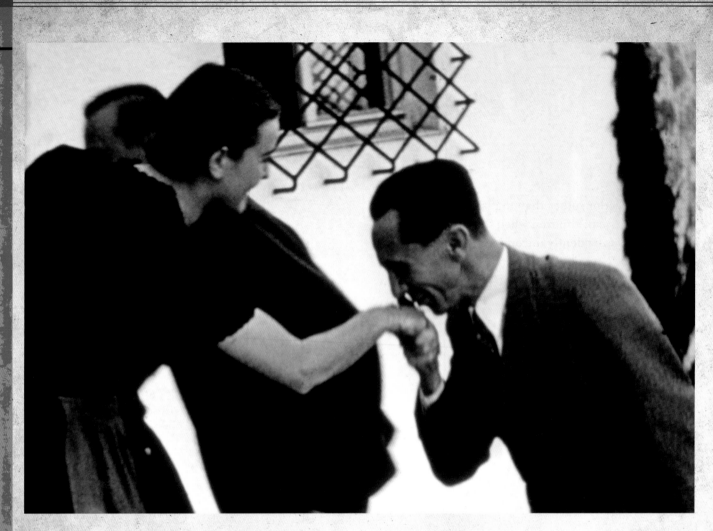

Eva Braun (with darkened hair) and Josef Goebbels at the Berghof

At the time he excused himself by declaring that he was 'married to the Reich'. He told Riefenstahl, 'marriage would plunge me into a sea of responsibilities that would turn me away from my main responsibilities that I owe to my people. To say the least, the decisions I would have to take would be such that I would not be allowed the slightest error. If things should turn sour, I would not accept it and there would be one exit only: a bullet in my head.'

In truth, only the most anodyne and undemanding females were perceived by him as not posing a threat. He considered young pretty women to be merely decorative and once remarked that 'a highly intelligent man should take a primitive and stupid woman'.

But he venerated the archetypal Aryan mother who sacrificed her own happiness to bear more blue-eyed blond babies for the Fatherland and doubtless saw his own doting mother in such a light.

SHALLOW NATURE

Eva Braun was neither a heroine nor a matriarch, but she was devoted, patient and undemanding; and physically the picture of healthy Aryan maidenhood,

Not the kind of girl who would seduce the hero in Hitler's Wagnerian fantasy world and drain his vitality so that he would be unable to fulfil his sacred mission. Or worse, infect the knights of the New Order with the 'social disease' that might have been the source of Hitler's fear of intimacy.

Albert Speer may have been right when he remarked that, 'For all writers of history, Eva Braun is going to be a disappointment.'

The middle daughter of a Munich schoolmaster, Eva was by all accounts a shallow, self-obsessed young woman who became a companion to the most powerful man in Europe primarily because she was compliant, obedient and satisfied to be by his side.

She had to be servile, emotionally immature and slavishly devoted to have endured his indifference, both physically and emotionally. Who else but a foolishly romantic overgrown schoolgirl would have suffered the humiliations he subjected her to without complaint, which included being confined to her room whenever important guests were expected, abstaining from using make-up, dressing in shapeless, plain, unfeminine clothes, refraining from smoking in his presence and being forbidden from cavorting in 'provocative' swimwear while performing her daily exercises?

HOW THEY MET

It seems that Hitler felt threatened by women who flaunted their sexuality and frowned upon any active display of affection, other than that shown to his dog Blondi or small children when the cameras were turning. He was evidently uncomfortable with physical closeness of any kind – it was said that he couldn't bear being touched – and tolerated Eva because she was content to bask in his shadow and patiently await those rare moments when they could be alone. He was a petty bourgeois and an insufferable prude, but the allure and exhilaration of power evidently compensated her for the lack of a normal physical relationship.

Those who knew her well considered her pleasant but not too bright. She had demonstrated no particular aptitude for academic subjects while at her convent school, distinguishing herself only in athletics, an interest with which she occupied herself in later life when not playing hostess or shopping for clothes.

Having left the convent without qualifications, she was fortunate to find employment as a secretary in the offices of the Nazi Party's official photographer, Heinrich Hoffmann. It was there in 1929 that she met Hitler, who was more than 20 years her senior. She was then just 17. Hoffmann described her as 'just an attractive little thing, in whom, in spite of her inconsequential and feather-brained outlook, he found the type of relaxation and repose he sought'. Hitler's attitude towards her can be gleaned from the fact that on those very rare occasions when he bought her jewellery, it was ostentatious and cheap.

LOYAL UNTIL DEATH

She accepted that their relationship had to be kept secret because he feared he would lose his female admirers if they knew of her existence, but even Eva had her limits and in 1932 she made a desperate bid for his attention by shooting herself in the throat.

Ironically, despite the lack of respect and affection that she had suffered, she proved the most loyal companion. While Goering, Himmler, Speer, Bormann and many of his most trusted acolytes tried to save their own skins, Eva Braun ended her futile and fruitless life by Hitler's side.

EVA BRAUN

BORN: 6 February, 1912, Munich, Bavaria
DIED: 30 April, 1945, Berlin
NICKNAME: The Rolleiflex girl

Family: Father: Friedrich 'Fritz' Braun (schoolteacher); mother: Franziska 'Fanny' Kronberger (seamstress); siblings: Ilse and Margarete (Eva was second daughter); husband (if only for a short time): Adolf Hitler

Life: Educated at Catholic institute; became assistant to Nazi photographer Heinrich Hoffmann, then photographer after 1933; met Adolf Hitler in 1929; suicide attempts in 1932 and 1935, perhaps to gain Hitler's attention; Hitler provided Munich apartment, 1935, villa 1936; part of Berghof household, 1936 onwards, also given apartment at Reich Chancellery; marriage and suicide, 1945

Description: Seen as shallow, colourless; fond of sports and dancing; relationship with Hitler hidden, even occupied separate rooms to Hitler at Berghof; sex life with Hitler subject of speculation; took many photographs/films of Berghof guests; very fond of her Scottish Terriers; fanatically devoted to Hitler

'From our first meeting I swore to follow you anywhere – even unto death – I live only for your love.' Eva Braun in letter to Hitler

Hitler's nurse Erna Flegel, who remained in the bunker in Berlin to the bitter end, remembered her as 'a completely colourless personality' who wouldn't have stood out among a crowd of stenographers. 'She didn't have any importance. She wasn't really his wife.'

Erna remembers that the death of Hitler's dog affected the survivors more than that of Eva Braun.

EVA AND ADOLF

› Eva's private photo album contains a picture of her in blackface and dressed as jazz singer Al Jolson.

› In Hitler's first will, made on 2 May 1938, he left her a legacy that would provide the equivalent of 600 pounds a year, to be paid until her death.

› Knowledge of Hitler's mistress was kept from the German public and even visitors to the Berghof assumed she was one of the Führer's private secretaries. Her name was deliberately omitted from the telephone directory at the Führer's Alpine retreat.

› She was snubbed by all but two of the Nazi wives (Henriette von Schirach and Margarete Speer) and amused herself by swimming, exercising and shopping, her favourite purchase being Ferragamo shoes.

› Hitler committed suicide using the same pistol his niece had killed herself with 17 years earlier.

› After their suicide their incompletely cremated bodies were recovered by the advancing Russians and taken to Magdeburg, where they were buried until being exhumed and destroyed in 1970. During the journey to Magdeburg the Soviet troops buried the bodies each night, then dug them up again in the morning.

When this picture was taken on 1 January 1930, Eva Braun would have been just 17 and Adolf Hitler 40

Adolf Eichmann

The Hollow Man

'I will gladly jump into my grave in the knowledge that five million enemies of the Reich have already died like animals.'

The balding man in the glass booth sat impassively behind thick, black-framed spectacles, smartly dressed in a plain suit and tie. His high forehead, receding hair and expressionless face betrayed no emotion as the first of more than a hundred witnesses took the stand just a few feet from him to relive the nightmares that would haunt them to the grave. He might have been an official in a government department, rubber-stamping documents as they passed across his desk, instead of a notorious war criminal on trial for genocide.

As the television cameras broadcast the day's proceedings from the stifling heat of the Jerusalem courtroom, Adolf Eichmann remained a 'block of ice', in the words of one former inmate.

SMILING AT DEATH

He made careful notes with the air of a man who wanted to be sure that everything was in order, but otherwise he appeared detached, remote from the proceedings as if recording the fortunes of another defendant entirely. He seemed to be resigned to his fate, having accepted that it was now too late for Germany to order his extradition and save him from the death penalty. Only once did he betray his true feelings. When the court lights were dimmed and newsreel film of the liberation of Bergen-Belsen was projected on to a screen, a young television technician caught a close-up of the defendant on a monitor. He was smiling.

The former Obersturmbannführer (Lieutenant-Colonel) had been indicted on 15 counts including Crimes Against Humanity and Crimes Against the

ADOLF EICHMANN

BORN: 19 March, 1906, Solingen, Germany

DIED: 31 May, 1962, Ramla, Israel

NICKNAME: The Bloodhound

Family: Father: businessman/industrialist Adolf Eichmann; mother: Maria Schefferling; married to Vera Liebl, 1935; sons Klaus, Horst, Dieter, Ricardo

Career/life: Left high school without graduating, worked in various jobs; joined SS in 1932; transferred to SS Jewish Department, 1934; Transport Administrator, Final Solution, 1942; escaped to Austria, 1944; captured by US Army, escaped 1946; sailed to Argentina, 1950; captured by Mossad, 1960; tried in Jerusalem, 1961; executed, 1962

Description: Unremarkable, even non-existent, personality; no apparent feelings of guilt at trial; claimed to have no strong anti-Jewish feelings; took great satisfaction in bureaucratic efficiency; seen by some as typical psychopath

'To sum it all up, I must say that I regret nothing.'

Jewish People, all of which he denied. He was accused of co-ordinating the deportation of Jews from all over Europe to extermination camps and confiscating the property and assets of those he had sent to their deaths.

NO PERSONALITY

Even in the glare of worldwide publicity, Eichmann remained an enigma. Not because he exuded an air of mystery, but because he projected no personality at all. He was a colourless two-dimensional man, blank, expressionless and seemingly disconnected from reality.

When he did speak it was to deny all responsibility and to claim that he had never been an anti-Semite. After all, hadn't he once had a Jewish mistress?

It was common knowledge among his colleagues in the Gestapo's Bureau of Jewish Affairs in Berlin that he had cheated on his wife with a series of mistresses, one of whom he took on a 'working holiday' to Hungary, where he supervised the rounding up and deportation of Jews to Dachau and Auschwitz. Witnesses testified that he often strutted before his intended victims, assuring them that Auschwitz was a 'holiday camp' which only married couples were eligible to enter. So they had better get wed if they didn't want to lose their place. He even penned postcards for inmates to sign and send to their relatives, urging them to hurry and join the rest of the family.

CUNNING COVER-UP

Not long before he was abducted by the Mossad – the Israeli Institute for Intelligence and Special Operations – in 1960, and smuggled out of Argentina, Eichmann had entertained an ex-member of the Waffen SS, Willem Sassen, and agreed to talk at length about his crucial role in the Holocaust. The so-called 'Sassen

The balding man in the glass booth: Adolf Eichmann betrayed very little emotion during his trial in Jerusalem

INSIDE THE MIND OF EICHMANN

Eichmann's Jewish mistress had been married to an SS officer who divorced her when her ancestry was revealed. He was the only Nazi to have learned Hebrew, but he admitted he had 'exaggerated' his fluency to impress his superiors.

Prior to his trial, Eichmann was examined by Israeli psychiatrist I.S. Kulcsar, who conducted a series of interviews and tests. These revealed an obsessive–compulsive personality, who continually struggled against violent emotions at the core of his being. Kulcsar also studied Eichmann's biography and discovered no evidence of blind obedience to authority. On the contrary, as a boy he had skipped school and later joined the Nazi Party against his father's wishes. He had grown up in a middle-class Protestant family with no history of psychiatric disorders and yet he had exhibited a preoccupation with suicide. On one occasion he had defied an order not to go into the streets during an air-raid. His intelligence was average, his worldview unfeeling, his outlook fatalistic and 'superficially logical', and he was plagued by fear and guilt in relation to problems with sex and unrestrained aggression.

It was Kulcsar's opinion that Eichmann was 'driven by archaic, uncontrollable forces, leading him to sheer destruction and hatred of all life'. Unable to control these inner drives, he had joined a violent political group which manifested the same destructive and manipulative personality as his own. But his 'homicidal urge persisted' and effectively possessed him for the remainder of his life.

The test results were sent to Hungarian-born psychiatrist Léopold Szondi for blind analysis, along with the results from other unidentified subjects so that there could be no risk of prejudice. Szondi reported that of the 6,000 cases he had studied this one was unique. The anonymous subject exhibited 'unprecedented murderous tendencies', 'ambivalent sexual tendencies', a 'strong sadomasochistic syndrome', a 'predisposition for incriminating others' and an 'undisciplined autistic ego', which manifests as 'an insatiable drive for power without regard for the limits of reality'. In addition, Szondi identified a latent 'evil, homicidal impulse of great intensity' and concluded: 'This man is a criminal with an insatiable killing intention. His public danger is still increased by the autistic power-ego and the tendency to projection.'

It was Szondi's belief that objective psychoanalysis cannot be used to trace the origins of an 'evil' personality, because the causes are not to be found in the subjects' abusive childhood but in the nature of their being, which causes them to have a distorted perception of the truth from birth.

However there is one clue as to why Eichmann may have harboured such an all-consuming hatred for the Jews. As a boy he had been taunted by other children who called him 'the little Jew', because of his Semitic appearance. In his mind he may have convinced himself that if he could be seen to have eliminated Jews from public life, he couldn't be accused of being one.

So being a cynical opportunist he learned Hebrew and attended Jewish social gatherings to ingratiate himself with the people he intended to eradicate from German culture and society and, by doing so, further his career in the regime.

tapes' reveal that Eichmann and his superiors were not only exceptionally callous but also cunning and devious in covering up the nature and enormity of their crimes.

'We had words for the concealment of annihilation such as "special treatment" or "expulsion to the east" or "the final solution to the Jewish question".' It was Orwellian doublespeak taken to hideous extremes.

And he would justify whatever atrocities he presided over by quoting the SS oath, which demanded unquestioning obedience and loyalty. When asked if that meant he would murder his own father if ordered to do so, he didn't hesitate to reply 'yes'.

ENJOYED HIS WORK

He told Sassen that he enjoyed his work and was proud of having been an efficient administrator. 'I must confess I did not greet this assignment with the apathy of an ox. I was fascinated by it.' And on the witness stand he declared, 'My heart was light and joyful in my work, because the decisions were not mine.'

But at his trial he denied being the architect of the 'Final Solution'. That 'honour', he said, went to General Reinhard Heydrich, head of the Reich Main Security Office and Hitler's personal favourite.

Eichmann attempted to portray himself as nothing

more than a 'transportation officer', whose duties were confined to logistics. He was the man who made the trains run on time. It was immaterial to him that these engines pulled cattle trucks loaded with human cargo bound for the death camps. And when he was admonished by his superiors for packing twice as many people into one particular train than was usual, he explained that it was of no concern because many of them were children and didn't take up so much space.

In private Eichmann had shared his colleagues' pride in facilitating the eradication of the Jews from Germany and the conquered territories to the east. He boasted to Sassen that he had dictated Goering's letter to Heydrich on 31 July 1941, ordering the genocide of the Jews. 'I dictated the letter. They are my words. The letter was drafted by us. It was only signed by Goering.' But in court with the eyes of the world fixed upon him, he denied being a significant part of the machinery.

As a functionary he was commendably thorough and methodical. His own colleagues had described him as a 'tyrant', which he took as a compliment saying, 'It wasn't my business to be loved.' No detail was too small to escape his attention.

Not a single Jew was to escape his trap. Whenever he received an appeal urging him to make an exception because a particular individual was of use to another department, Eichmann would refuse point blank to release them.

He told Sassen, 'One of these officers was a certain Obergruppenführer Wolff, whom I once wanted to challenge to a duel because he made a swine of me over the telephone. He wanted to grant a particular Jew an extraordinary status, and this I could not allow under any circumstances. If I were to make exceptions which were not covered by the Reichsführer's instructions, it would have started an avalanche.'

Eichmann (second from right) looks on approvingly as Nazi officers cut a Jewish prisoner's hair at the horrendous Bergen-Belsen concentration camp

HISTORY RE-WRITTEN

When not in court, he spent the long hours of solitude in his cell writing his memoirs in which he absolved himself of all blame and expressed the hope that he might persuade the judges to be lenient. But after handing down the verdict of 'Guilty' on all counts and passing the sentence of death, the judges ordered the papers to be locked away where they remained unseen for 40 years. Adolf Eichmann was hanged just after midnight on 31 May 1962.

His memoirs portray a vain, arrogant, unrepentant personality with a weakness for self-aggrandizement and a habit of rewriting history – casting himself in the role of a courageous man of principle. When offered false papers to aid his escape at the end of the war, he claimed to have spat on them in disdain and waved his revolver as the only 'certificate' he would need to show his captors.

An unabashed fantasist, he confided to Sassen that he had offered to lead a last stand against the Allies in the Alpine stronghold around Berchtesgaden. And that SS General Ernst Kaltenbrunner had commended him for his selfless gesture and sacrifice.

'Now [Himmler] can talk to Eisenhower differently in his negotiations, for he will know that if Eichmann is in the mountains he will never surrender...'

Sensing that he had the ear of a gullible admirer, Eichmann added, 'My immediate superior, General Müller, said to me, "If we had 50 Eichmanns we could have won the war!!"'

This recasting of himself as a man of action was disputed by SS Captain Dieter Wisliceny, a key figure in the deportation and liquidation of Hungarian Jews, who

described Eichmann as 'a cowardly man, who was at great pains to protect himself from responsibility'.

INSTIGATED 'DEATH MARCH'

Eichmann's capacity for self-deception however, was limitless. After witnessing a mass execution, he asked the readers of his memoirs to see him as a 'sensitive man' forced to steel himself into committing 'unpalatable' acts.

> 'At heart I am a very sensitive man. I simply can't look at any suffering without trembling myself. Even if today I see someone with a deep cut, I have to look away.'

But the earlier confession captured on the Sassen tapes has Eichmann bragging that it was he who suggested the camps use Zyklon-B gas instead of carbon monoxide to speed up the killings. He is alleged to have said, 'It has proven efficient at exterminating lice, so it should be good for exterminating human vermin.'

And it was Eichmann who instigated the 'Death March' of 50,000 Jews from Hungary to the Austrian border in 1944, in defiance of Himmler's express orders, because Eichmann wouldn't allow the advancing Russians to thwart his plans. After having repeatedly denied knowing anything about the forced 137-mile (220-km) march of starving men, women and children, Eichmann finally identified his signature on a document produced by the Israeli prosecutors, ordering the march in defiance of Himmler's directive. Pride and arrogance had proved his undoing. His obsession with eliminating the last Jews from Hungary had been so all-consuming that he had defied an order from Himmler to ensure that the last 'consignment' of Jews were gassed before the Russians entered Budapest.

> 'I was responsible for the march. I admit it. As it turned out, the march was more trouble than if I had sent a hundred trains to Auschwitz. I wanted to show the Allies my hand, as it were, to tell them, "You smashed our transportation routes, but we will carry on in the most elegant manner."'

Never once during his detention did he express remorse. 'They were old people. It is clear when you chop wood, chips will fall.'

His only regret was that he hadn't murdered more.

> 'We didn't do our job properly. We could have done more. I didn't just take orders. If I had been that kind of person, I would have been a fool. Instead, I was part of the thinking process, I was an idealist.'

Eichmann helped select the site for the gas chambers at Auschwitz

Godfathers of Nazism

....

The Nazi Party's Unlikely Beginnings

'This absurd little organization with its few members seemed to me to possess the one advantage that it had not frozen into an "organization", but left the individual opportunity for real personal activity.'

Adolf Hitler

Adolf Hitler was unimpressed by his first sight of the German Workers' Party. It was a ragged collective of disgruntled ex-soldiers, small shopkeepers and manual labourers who gathered in a back room of a Munich beer hall in the months following Germany's defeat in the Great War to bemoan their lot and argue about who was to blame for it.

GOING NOWHERE

The Party had been formed just nine months earlier on 5 January 1919, from the merger of two groups – the Committee of Independent Workmen and the Political Workers' Circle – in the aftermath of Germany's humiliating defeat and the abdication of the Kaiser. Its leaders Anton Drexler, a locksmith, Karl Harrer, a journalist, Gottfried Feder, an economist and Dietrich Eckart, a failed playwright feared that the new Weimar Republic was too weak to prevent their enemies, the communists, from seizing power. The DAP (Deutsche Arbeiterpartei) was not only opposed to capitalism but also to communism, which they referred to as 'the plague from the east' and which they imagined had been whipped up by a 'Jewish–Masonic conspiracy' led by Karl Marx.

But none of the Party's founding fathers had a gift for public speaking or for promoting their organization, which was indistinguishable from the dozens of radical political groups vying for votes in Bavaria in those dark and desperate days.

Of the four founders, only one – Dietrich Eckart – made a lasting impression on the future Führer that first night at the Sterneckerbräu beer keller. The others were quickly discarded after Hitler manoeuvred himself into a position to seize the leadership and use it as a platform for his virulent brand of extreme nationalism and anti-Semitism.

Hitler suggested adding 'National Socialist' to the German Workers' Party, redefining socialism to apply only to 'pure-blood Germans'

DREXLER, FEDER AND HARRER

'We agreed to meet on January 5th in a little eating-house in Munich... to found the Deutsche Arbeiter Partei.'

Drexler writing about Harrer

MUTUAL CONTEMPT

Hitler regarded Drexler with contempt because he had declared himself unfit to serve in the army during the war. In Hitler's opinion, Drexler was a poor leader, weak, uncertain and 'not fanatical enough'. The feeling was mutual. Drexler despised the 'Bohemian corporal' from the first, describing Hitler as 'an absurd little man'.

They should have found common ground, for their fanaticism had been fostered by frustration – Drexler had left his home in Munich to find work in Berlin, only to be 'humiliated' by having to play the zither on street corners for pfennigs, like a common beggar, and Hitler had left his village to eke out a pittance selling crude watercolours in Vienna and had ended up sleeping in a dosshouse.

When Hitler took over as leader in late 1921, Drexler was compensated with the title of Honorary Chairman, but he had no say in policy-making and left the Party after the Munich Putsch, dying in obscurity in 1942.

OLD-FASHIONED IDEAS

Hitler thought more of Gottfried Feder, a former construction company owner who had taken up economics with the zeal of an evangelist. It was Feder's speech on 'Interest slavery' at that first meeting which persuaded Hitler that there was potential in the Party.

As he related in *Mein Kampf*, 'After I had heard Feder's first lecture, the thought flashed through my head that I had found the essential suppositions for the founding of a new Party. The development of Germany was clear enough to show me that the hardest battles of the future were to be fought not against enemy nations,

TOP: Anton Drexler

BOTTOM: Gottfried Feder

but against international capitalism. I felt a powerful prophecy of this coming battle in Feder's lecture.'

But after Hitler was appointed Chancellor in 1933, Feder's ideas were considered 'old-fashioned' and naïve. His plan to break up large estates into smaller plots to serve the nearby cities, making them autonomous and self-sufficient, was opposed by rich landowners and industrialists, who persuaded Hitler and his new economic adviser Hjalmar Schacht that it was impractical. Feder was given the nominal position of Undersecretary in the Reich Ministry of Economics and resigned as soon as he realized that he had lost all influence with the Party. He continued to preach his doctrine of rurbanization, or rural–urban fusion, as a lecturer until his death in September 1941.

HITLER GAINS LEADERSHIP

Harrer and Drexler had been members of the Thule Society, a study group primarily concerned with proving the superiority of the Aryan race and its antediluvian origins in Atlantis. Harrer had no political ambitions and was opposed to the Party becoming an active political force in the Bavarian republic. He had formed the DAP as a radical discussion group limited to seven members, which is why Hitler's membership number was altered from 55 to 7 to give the impression that he had been a founding member and initiate of the original inner circle. Even Drexler had scornfully referred to the DAP in its first incarnation as the 'Harrer Society', while Hitler criticized it for being 'the worst kind of club'. Desperate to build the back room

LEFT: Sketch of journalist Heinrich Harrer

BELOW: The Thule Society emblem: they believed in the coming of a German Messiah who would restore Germany to its former glory

1 9 1 9

Thule-Gesellschaft

debating society into a real political force, Hitler used his gift for propaganda and organization to inundate the Party with new members loyal to himself, so that when the crucial vote came he could wrest the leadership from its unassertive founders. By early 1920 he had generated sufficient support and Harrer was forced to concede the leadership. Harrer continued to edit the Nazi newspaper, the *Münchener Beobachter*, but died six years later, apparently of 'natural causes'.

Anton Drexler (with moustache and swastika armband) at a meeting of the NSDAP in a Munich beer hall: Feder can be seen immediately behind him and there are bouncers on hand to deal with any trouble

Hitler then surrounded himself with ardent admirers who were not drawn from the working and lower middle class and did not share the values of the original members. Chief among these was Dietrich Eckart.

DIETRICH ECKART
Hitler's Soul Mate

*'Follow Hitler! He will dance,
but it is I who have called
the tune.'*

Dietrich Eckart fancied himself as the rustic poet and braggart in Ibsen's *Peer Gynt* (a play he had translated for the German stage), a rough and ready fellow esteemed by his hard-drinking friends for his jovial manner and stock of humorous stories. Fellow Party members recalled the stocky, short-necked playwright looking like 'an old walrus' with his small beady eyes framed in shell-rimmed glasses and large balding head. His gruff, rasping voice rolled out like thunder when he railed against those he blamed for Germany's misfortunes, but it made him sound positively avuncular when he was in good humour.

REVERED BY HITLER

It was said that Eckart had the enthusiasm to start an entire movement by himself, but hadn't the stamina to see it through. And this is why Hitler seized the opportunity to take over the NSDAP once he had the measure of the members and had figured out how to sideline their leaders. But he revered Eckart who he referred to as his 'fatherly friend', honouring the old man's memory with a bust in the Reich Chancellery after he had assumed power and naming the Olympic stadium in Berlin in his honour.

It was Eckart who brought together the diverse elements of the Party's core followers – the small businessmen, the paramilitary members of the Freikorps and the unskilled workers – under one banner. They had one aim – to expose the 'Jewish Bolshevik conspiracy' they blamed for all their ills.

HITLER'S COACH

But Eckart offered more than moral support when Hitler succumbed to black moods of doubt and depression in the early days of 'the struggle',

particularly after the region's political leaders had banned him from speaking so as not to provoke the Bavarian authorities into imposing martial law on the eve of the planned putsch in 1923.

Eckart coached his protégé in the art of public speaking, corrected his grammar and spelling and toned down his polemics for publication. And it was Eckart who persuaded Hitler to contain his loathing for the ruling classes and make himself more presentable in order to court the industrialists, financiers and upper classes whose support would prove crucial to the Party's fortunes. He also used his contacts in the theatre and publishing to introduce the uneducated provincial rabble-rouser to influential members of Munich society, whose financial contributions enabled the Party to fund their political campaigns.

Eckart persuaded Hitler that the only sure road to power was via the ballot box and not by backstreet brawling or armed revolt, which would only provoke the administration in Berlin to intervene.

Until Hitler met Eckart, the former Bohemian corporal was a martyr to a turmoil of violent emotions; resentment, regret and antagonism boiled within him, leaving him to rant at unseen enemies and intangible forces which he believed had been responsible for opposing his entry into the art academy in Vienna. They were the same nebulous forces that had conspired to stab the German armed forces in the back in 1918, bringing the Great War to an ignominious end. It was Eckart who fed the flames of Hitler's anti-Semitism with fake documentary 'evidence' such as the notorious *Protocols of the Elders of Zion*, forged by Ludwig Müller von Hausen (or Sergey Nilus), and ridiculous fantasies concerning a global conspiracy orchestrated by the fictitious and supposedly omnipotent Illuminati.

DIETRICH ECKART

BORN: 23 March, 1868, Neumarkt, Upper Palatinate, Bavaria
DIED: 26 December, 1923, Berchtesgaden, Upper Bavaria
NICKNAME: Nazism's Spiritual Father

Family: Father: Christian Eckart, royal notary and lawyer; mother: Anna; wife: Rosa Marx-Wiedeburg

Career/life: Abandoned medical studies to become poet and journalist, then wrote a number of plays, mostly without success; joined Thule Society, 1913; edited *Auf gut deutsch*, anti-Semitic publication, 1918–20; fervent critic of Weimar Republic, leading to becoming founder member of NSDAP, 1919; became Hitler's friend and mentor; editor-in-chief of the *Völkischen Beobachter*, 1921; arrested after Munich Putsch, died shortly afterwards at Berchtesgaden; revered by Hitler, who honoured him after his death in several ways

Description: Portly, wore a moustache or a neatly trimmed beard and dressed conventionally. In his later years and going bald, looked more like a bank clerk than a dreamer and revolutionary

'I believe in Hitler; above him there hovers a star.'

KINDRED SPIRITS

Eckart shared several significant character traits with his protégé which bound them together and led the Nazi leader to dedicate *Mein Kampf* to the man he called his 'North Star'. It appears that both men had what can only be described as a neurotic disposition. Feelings of rejection and intense anxiety had triggered a nervous breakdown in Eckart when he was separated from a girl he wanted to marry and Hitler suffered a similar psychosomatic crisis, which his doctors identified as 'hysterical blindness', after he was gassed at the end of the war.

Their temperaments were also uncannily alike. Both were volatile, dogmatic and apt to turn on anyone who dared to criticize or disagree with them. They each felt alienated and victimized and believed themselves to be superior to their own teachers and academics in general, whom they despised for having demonstrated the self-discipline and intelligence needed to acquire formal qualifications, qualities that neither man possessed. When Hitler was told that Eckart had dropped out of law school he tellingly remarked that his friend had done so 'so as not to become the perfect imbecile'. Instead, they put their faith in eccentric völkisch visionaries such as Lanz von Liebenfels and Guido von List and crank 'philosophers' who fostered the myth of Aryan superiority, which declared that Germans were a master race descended from giants who had survived the sinking of Atlantis.

Both men had been sickly children who lost their doting mothers at an early age and were embittered by the experience. Both of their fathers were strict authoritarians, arrogant in the extreme and scornful of those they considered beneath them. Eckart often found himself siding with the criminals brought before his father, a district magistrate who was in the habit of enforcing the letter rather than the spirit of the law.

Furthermore, both Hitler and Eckart had left their poor rural villages in the hope of finding artistic success and recognition in the big city (Hitler as an architect and artist, Eckart as a poet and playwright) and both were crushed when those ambitions were dashed. Neither could accept that they lacked the talent required to be successful and instead they blamed others for denying them what they believed was their birthright, their destiny.

DRIVEN BY MORPHINE

While still in his twenties Eckart became addicted to morphine, possibly to ease his bouts of manic depression and remained dependent until his death. According to Alfred Rosenberg, 'Without his sweet poison he could not live and applied the whole cunning of a possessor of this craving to get dose after dose.' His addiction affected his judgement and he began to read the writings of erratic philosophers

ECKART DOSSIER

› After his father's death Eckart lavished his inheritance on fine living, importing coffee from South America which he had freshly ground every morning and smoking up to fifteen cigars a day.

› Eckart's contribution to the Nazis' rise to power was, in Hitler's assessment, 'inestimable' and led to the failed playwright and poet having his portrait hung in a prominent position in the Munich Braunhaus and a bust placed in the Reich Chancellery, as well as having the Berlin Olympic stadium named in his honour.

› Eckart earned 1,000 marks for writing a four-line advertising 'jingle' for 'gout water', but refused to earn his living as a copywriter because he thought it wasn't worthy of his talent.

› His own father had him committed to a sanatorium to fight his morphine addiction. Years later Eckart checked himself into an asylum to detoxify himself and staged his plays with other inmates cast in the leading roles.

› In 1911 Eckart acted as a publicist for a con man who claimed to be the reincarnation of a German tribal leader.

› Eckart wrote the lyrics for the Nazi marching song 'Germany Awake'.

› Shortly before his death Eckart wrote a virulent anti-Semitic tract *Bolshevism: from Moses to Lenin*, which comprised an imaginary conversation between the author and his friend Adolf Hitler.

Early Nazis, 1922, among them Julius Streicher (fourth from left, front row) in his 'Marching and Chowder Club' on his Nuremberg estate.

and pseudo-intellectuals such as Ernst Haeckel, Otto Weininger and Gougenot des Mousseaux. Mousseaux had argued that Jews were the progeny of demons and predicted that they would wreak havoc in Germany before being 'put in their place'.

Having failed to be accepted by intellectuals and high society, Eckart turned on them, publishing virulent anti-Semitic diatribes in his tabloid scandal sheet *Auf gut deutsch*. His initial fascination with the Jews, whom he had seen as 'exotic', now became an unhealthy obsession. Like Hitler, he used the Jews as a scapegoat for his own personal failure and for the nation's troubles.

'They stand apart with their superior cleverness and ambition,' he wrote. 'We must always brandish the hammer if we don't want to become the anvil.'

Just three years after welcoming Hitler to the Party Eckart was dead, burned out by alcoholism and morphine addiction. His last words were prophetic.

'Do not mourn me for I shall have influenced history more than any other German.'

Hermann Goering

The 'Fat Man's' Taste for Excess

*'I am what I have always been,
the last Renaissance man,
if I may be allowed to say so.'*

When Hermann Goering handed himself over to the US 36th Infantry Division on a snow-blocked road near Radstadt, Austria on 7 May 1945, he was travelling in style in a five-ton Mercedes-Benz 540K with bullet-proof glass, steel-reinforced body and a set of plump suitcases strapped to the roof.

His entourage consisted of some twenty vehicles and with him were his wife, his sister-in-law, his daughter, General von Epp (Gauleiter of Austria), his chef, valet and butler, plus assorted aides and bodyguards – in total about 75 people. But compared to the previous heady decade of licentious living, the Reichsmarschall was suddenly down to 'the bare necessities'.

Stowed away in his baggage was a vast stash of pills to see him through any emergency. By 1937 Goering was heavily addicted to codeine, a substance present in painkillers and cough tablets. It's thought that, as the war neared its end, he could have been taking up to 100 pills a day. It's also believed that he might have been on methadone, a synthetic opiate developed by Nazi chemists during the war when opium supplies from the Far East dried up. After years of debauchery, he tipped the scales at over 300 lb (136 kg). But as Gustave Gilbert, the prison psychologist at Nuremberg, said,

> '...His drug abuse probably came down to guilt from the mass extermination! Goering wasn't one to suffer acute anxiety, but his perverted sense of values had certain limits...'

ON THE SS DEATH LIST

Shortly before his suicide in the bunker, it seems that Hitler, once Goering's staunchest supporter, had removed him from all positions of power, accused him of treachery and ordered the SS to track him down. At any rate that's what *Der Dicke* (the 'Fat Man', as he was affectionately known to the German public) believed, and so he had become wary, particularly with so many jumpy SS men around in the aftermath of defeat.

Above all, he was determined to avoid the terrible fate of falling into the hands of the advancing Russians. That was why he sent his senior aide Oberst Von Brauchitsch to the Americans to negotiate his surrender after a ceasefire had been agreed.

US Lieutenant Jerome Shapiro volunteered to go 80 miles (129 km) behind enemy lines on a top-secret mission to arrest the 'highest-ranking Nazi' and organizer of the 'Final Solution' to kill all Jews. Shapiro, himself a Jew, reports coming across Goering and his household and requesting Goering's sidearm in surrender. Goering offered not only to unload the Smith & Wesson service pistol, but presented Shapiro with his gold-plated Walther PPK. However dire the situation, he never forgot the value of strategic gifts in helping him work his way into the good books of those who could prove useful. But now he was no longer moving in exalted circles.

In a gaudy coat of his own design, Goering at a military exhibition in Vienna in 1941 with General Wilhelm List on his left

HERMANN GOERING

BORN: 12 January , 1893, Rosenheim, Bavaria
DIED: 15 October, 1946, Nuremberg, Bavaria
NICKNAME: The Iron Knight, *Der Dicke*

Family: Father: Heinrich Ernst Goering (First Governor-General of German Protectorate of South West Africa); mother: Franziska; siblings: Albert, Karl, Paula, Olga (he was fourth of five children); wives: Emmy and Carin (died 1931); daughter: Edda

Career/life: WWI fighter pilot and ace; wounded in the Munich Putsch, 1923; stunt pilot; founded the Gestapo in 1933; appointed Commander-in-Chief of the Luftwaffe, 1935; became Reichsmarschall, 1940; designated Hitler's successor, 1941; convicted of crimes against humanity at Nuremberg and sentenced to death

Description: Loved ostentation and being the centre of attention; was said to change his uniform 'five times a day'; once transferred to a padded cell in a Swedish asylum after trying to strangle a nurse; relentless appetite for food, drink, money, art and luxury; when he fell out of favour he retreated into self-indulgence and drug addiction; expert at soliciting bribes, blackmail, industrial surveillance and wiretapping; drug addict

Proud boast: *'I intend to go down in history as a great man. In 50 to 60 years, there will be statues of Hermann Goering all over Germany.'*

HAPPY HOUR

Captivity began well for Goering. On 12 May US General Carl Spaatz invited him to a 'cocktail hour' at Kitzbuehl which lasted late into the night. Over a bottle of whisky and huge portions of food, the two men, both ex-First World War air aces, cracked jokes and exchanged stories about wartime.

Goering proved to be a very jovial guest indeed, playing the accordion, singing patriotic songs at the drop of a hat and drinking fellow revellers under the table. But it was to be his last taste of freedom. Soon he was taken away and he found himself behind bars.

HITLER'S SWASHBUCKLING DEPUTY

> *'What do I care about danger? I've sent soldiers and airmen to death against the enemy – why should I be afraid?'*

Hermann Goering was frequently depicted in Allied newspaper cartoons as a flamboyant, blustering buffoon, strutting the world stage in a series of ostentatious uniforms like a Ruritanian prince in a comic operetta. But although he was notorious for awarding himself medals and for glorifying in the official titles Hitler bestowed upon him, the former First World War flying ace was no fool. Nor was he ever considered a figure of fun by those who feared his volatile temper and his vindictive cruelty.

Born in Marienbad, Bavaria in 1893, Goering was the fourth of five children, three being from their father's first marriage. His father was a former cavalry officer and Consul General and his mother a farmer's daughter, but Goering was raised as an aristocrat thanks to the generosity of his mother's lover, who allowed her and the boy to live in one of two castles that he owned on the Austrian border.

During the early months of the First World War Goering served in the infantry, but was transferred to the air force in 1915 and became an ace in Manfred von Richthofen's JG1 squadron, earning the Iron Cross and the Pour le Mérite. After von Richthofen's death, Goering became squadron leader and ended the war with 15 kills to his credit.

His marriage to Swedish Baroness Carin von Krantzow in February 1923 bought him into the social whirl of the German nobility, which was to prove invaluable when he later sought funding for the Nazi Party and Hitler's endorsement by the ruling classes.

RUTHLESS RISE TO POWER

Restless and impatient for action, Goering had joined the nascent Nazi Party in 1922 not out of any revolutionary or political ideals, but to combat communism in the beer halls and backstreets by breaking a few heads and strong-arming those who voiced dissent at Party meetings. Within a year he had been appointed head of the SA (the paramilitary wing of the Nazis) and was in the front ranks on the march through Munich during the failed Beer Hall Putsch of 1923. Wounded in the leg and groin, Goering fled to Austria and soon became addicted to morphine, though he claimed to have kicked the habit two years later.

An amnesty allowed him to return to Germany in 1926, where he rose to power as Hitler's second-in-command. He was appointed President of the Reichstag in 1932 when the Nazis became the major party in the German parliament. Rudolf Hess held the official title of Deputy Führer from 1933 until his ill-fated flight to Britain in May 1941, when Hitler stripped him of it, but Goering had already been appointed Hitler's successor.

Goering on trial at Nuremberg when he looked slim for the first time in years and, clear of drugs, his mind was once again formidable

It is believed that Goering conceived the idea of setting fire to the Reichstag in February 1933 so that the Nazis could seize power under the pretext that the communists were planning an armed revolution. Whether it was his idea or not, Goering was instrumental in consolidating the Nazis' grip on power and in rearming the military in spite of the restrictions imposed by the Versailles Treaty.

He was also responsible for founding the Gestapo, Germany's hated secret police force, and it was Goering who conceived the idea of concentration camps, which he attempted to justify by comparing them to the internment camps the British had constructed during the Boer War.

His ruthless determination to settle scores, no matter how old they might be, was revealed by the thoroughness with which he implemented the purging of the German High Command and the massacre of dissident elements in the SA, on the Night of the Long Knives in June 1934. These were acts for which he remained stubbornly unrepentant to the end.

As he said, 'Each bullet which leaves the barrel of a police pistol now is my bullet. If one calls this murder, then I have murdered; I ordered all this, I back it up. I assume the responsibility, and I am not afraid to do so.'

But Goering lost both face and favour after his much-vaunted Luftwaffe failed to win the Battle of Britain in the summer of 1940 and he retreated even further into the background after failing in his boast to be able to supply the besieged Sixth Army at Stalingrad, which saw the tide of the war turn in favour of the Allies.

CHEATING THE HANGMAN

Ironically, it was only after the war, when he stood trial at Nuremberg, that he once again demonstrated a sharp intellect and a magnetic presence (he scored 138 in an IQ test conducted by a prison psychiatrist). It was perhaps his most compelling public performance and one which earned him the grudging respect of many members of the prosecution and the press. Everyone knew that he would be found guilty and sentenced to hang and that this would be the last time he would command the world stage.

But Goering would not give the victors the satisfaction of executing him like a common criminal. On 15 October 1946 he committed suicide in his cell by biting into a capsule of cyanide that had allegedly been smuggled in to him by a sympathetic guard.

THE PORTLY ART PLUNDERER

> 'During a war, everybody loots a little bit. None of my so-called looting was illegal.'

Goering's mother predicted that her son would either be 'a great man or a great criminal'. Her assessment proved prophetic. At the conclusion of the Nuremberg trial in 1946 the Reichsmarschall was convicted on four counts: conspiracy to wage war, crimes against peace, war crimes and crimes against humanity, for which he was sentenced to death. The 'lesser' crime of looting was disregarded, despite Goering having ordered and organized the theft of some of the world's greatest art treasures in what must surely qualify as the crime of the century.

PERSONAL TREASURE HOUSE

His own 'appropriations' unit catalogued more than 4,000 liberated works of art, including 1,800 paintings by such masters as Matisse, Degas, Vermeer and Van Gogh, a haul estimated to be in excess of 20 per cent of the great art treasures of Europe. He had the finest pieces crated up and shipped off to furnish his imposing hunting lodge in the Schorfheide forest north of Berlin. Carinhall, named after his late first wife, also housed a private casino, an indoor swimming pool and two model train sets that took up the entire attic and basement

Goering takes questions from the Allied press corps, Nuremberg

space of approximately 400 square metres.

Visiting VIPs were invited to watch Goering playing with his trains, which travelled through Bavarian-styled model villages inhabited by figures including an SS man who waved at the passengers. For the climax of the demonstration Goering had fitted a model Stuka dive bomber above one of his model railway layouts and liked to send it down a wire to drop wooden bombs on to the moving trains.

Goering, it appears, still enjoyed playing with toys, but the art collection gave him particular pleasure. He told a prison psychiatrist at Nuremberg, 'I am so artistic in my temperament that masterpieces make me feel alive and glowing inside', yet he hung priceless masters haphazardly like cheap prints in a pawn shop. Some idea of the value of the collection can be gleaned from the fact that a single painting, Van Gogh's 'Portrait of Dr Gachet', was auctioned in 1990 for $82.5 million. But it was a mere fraction of the treasure Hitler had amassed for his planned Führermuseum, which was to have been built in Linz to commemorate the Third Reich's final victory over the Allies.

EARLY ACQUISITIONS

Goering began purchasing art in 1928, as soon as he was assured of a regular income from his post in the Reichstag. When the Nazis increased their grip on power and he was appointed President of the German parliament, he was able to seize priceless treasures from private collectors – who were threatened with imprisonment if they refused to sign over their property. As soon as the Nuremberg Laws were passed

Goering was one of the greatest art thieves of all time: here, an American soldier examines artworks stolen by the Nazis

he used them to confiscate art treasures from Jewish art dealers and wealthy families under the pretext that all Jews were enemies of the Reich and their property was forfeit. In 1943 these bills of sale were declared null and void by the British government, but it was already too late for the rightful owners, many of whom had been transported to extermination camps. To give his appropriations the veneer of legitimacy Goering would claim that certain paintings, statues or items of silverware were 'on loan', or he would ask the owner for an invoice that he had no intention of paying.

DAYLIGHT ROBBERY

The extent of the Nazis' rapacious plundering can be gleaned from the fact that Goebbels commissioned a 1,000-page inventory of the artworks to be taken from public galleries in France and that the ERR (*Einsatzstab Reichsleiter Rosenberg*) seized an estimated 22,000 objects of inestimable value from the conquered territories. The EER was set up to study the archaeological origins of the Aryan race but became an agency of the German Foreign Office which was authorized to seize rare manuscripts and books that might substantiate these theories – and burn those that didn't. By October 1944 1,418,000 railway wagons had been needed to ship the contents plundered from national libraries and archives, ecclesiastical authorities, Masonic lodges and private collections.

Once war was declared all pretence at legitimacy was unnecessary and the wholesale and open looting of art in the occupied territories was carried out by the Kunstschutz military corps under Goering's orders. Although national galleries and museums were stripped of their treasures on the pretext that they were being saved from Allied bombings, several curators in Italy and France risked their lives to make secret inventories of the stolen works, while members of the resistance followed the transports so that they could inform the Allies of the location of the stolen objects.

THE BITER BIT

Curiously, in the last days of the war Goering had exchanged many of the most valuable pieces by Impressionist painters for 'less degenerate' works which were of considerably lower value.

But a Dutch art dealer, Han van Meegeren, had the last laugh on 'the Fat Man'. In 1942 he persuaded Goering to part with 150 masterworks in exchange for a painting purporting to be by Jan Vermeer, but 'Christ and the Adulteress' has since been revealed to be a clever forgery. When Goering learned he had been fooled, a US official reported that 'he looked as if for the first time he had discovered there was evil in the world'.

Albert Goering

The Goering Who Rescued Jews

'He was always the exact opposite of me.
He wasn't interested in politics or the military, and I was.'

Hermann Goering

In Vienna the Brownshirts amused themselves by forcing Jews to scrub the pavements. It was guaranteed to draw a crowd who would jeer and shout abuse at the shopkeepers and neighbours they had silently despised for years. But on one street the SA thugs were confronted with a totally unaccustomed sight. An immaculately groomed gentleman in an expensive tailored suit stopped to kneel down beside the frightened women and began to scrub the stone slabs with a rag. He was hauled to his feet, but before they beat him they demanded to know his name. 'Goering,' he replied. 'Albert Goering. You must know my brother.'

Hermann Goering's younger brother took a special delight in provoking the Nazi thugs and watching their rage give way to incredulity then fear when he told them his name. He knew the Reichsmarschall could be relied upon to reduce them to gibbering wrecks when they phoned to confirm Albert's identity and that made their discomfort all the more pleasurable.

But it wasn't idle amusement that prompted Albert to play this dangerous game. He detested the Nazis for their stupidity as much as for their cruelty and the only way he could see of fighting back was to confront them and reveal them for what they were – backstreet bullies in uniform.

SHOWING COURAGE

The acts of compassion and courage that Albert exhibited demonstrated that the Nazi mind-set could not be attributed to nature or nurture but was a conscious act, the desire to conform and to indulge in one's basest instincts. It took a greater effort of will to resist being swept along on the wave of hysteria, to think and act independently. To do what is right, regardless of the risk.

It was rumoured that Albert was the result of an affair between Frau Goering and his Jewish godfather, Dr Hermann von Epenstein, whom he physically resembled, and that this accounted for his anti-Nazi attitude, but Frau Goering had been living abroad with her husband until the summer before Albert was born.

Albert's activities infuriated Hermann, who feared that his bitter rivals, Bormann and Himmler, would learn of his intervention on Albert's behalf and use it to undermine his authority and influence with Hitler. But Albert knew that Hermann relished throwing his weight about and dressing down his subordinates. Hermann had no love for Jews, but he must have secretly admired his brother's courage and panache.

FREEING PRISONERS

After 1934, when Hermann was relieved of his command over the Gestapo, it became more difficult to spring Albert from their clutches. But Albert was not easily intimidated. The German weekly news magazine

ALBERT GOERING

....

BORN: 9 March, 1895, Berlin, Germany
DIED: 20 December, 1966, Munich, West Germany

Family: Father: Heinrich Goering (but rumoured to be love child of Hermann von Epenstein); mother: Franziska (née Tiefenbrunn); siblings: Hermann, Karl, Paula, Olga; wives: Mila, a Czech, reputed to have married housekeeper just before death, also two other marriages; daughter: Elizabeth

Career/life: Began as film-maker with Oskar Pilzer; export director at Skoda works, where he engaged in anti-Nazi activities; tried at Nuremberg and eventually freed, then arrested by the Czechs and freed again; thereafter lived in straitened circumstances because of Goering name

Description: Tall, slim, cultured, charming and a Nazi-hater, almost the exact opposite of his brother Hermann

'Albert Göring used the power of his family name and pulled out all the stops, first to find out where my father was and then to make sure he was released immediately.' George Pilzer

After Anschluss in 1938, Jews were forced to scrub the pavements in Vienna as Nazi bullyboys looked on and mocked

CHALK AND CHEESE

> Hermann and Albert's godfather, Dr Hermann von Epenstein, invited the family to live in his medieval castles at Burg Veldenstein in Franconia and Burg Mauterndorf in the Austrian mountains, where meals were announced by a hunting horn, minstrels played for their entertainment and the servants were suitably dressed in medieval regalia.

> Hermann was sent to military school after cutting the strings of every stringed instrument in the school orchestra. Had he not been sent to cadet school he might have followed his younger brother's example.

> While awaiting trial at Nuremberg, Hermann told the American psychiatrist Leon Goldensohn that Albert and he were complete opposites in character and temperament. 'He was quiet, reclusive; I like crowds and company. He was melancholic and pessimistic, and I am an optimist. But he's not a bad fellow, Albert.'

> When Hermann fled to Sweden after the failed Munich Putsch, and became addicted to morphine, he refused to speak to his brother. Their silent feud lasted 12 years.

> Albert was ashamed of Hermann's involvement with the Nazis. He told his friend Albert Benbassat, 'I have a brother in Germany who is getting involved with that bastard Hitler. And he is going to come to a bad end if he continues that way.'

> To celebrate the Nazi annexation of Austria, Hermann Goering offered to grant each member of his family a wish. Albert asked for and obtained the release of Archduke Josef Ferdinand, who was being detained at Dachau.

Mauterndorf Castle in Austria where Hermann and Albert Goering were brought up

Der Spiegel reported that he rescued prisoners from the Terezin concentration camp in 1944 by driving up to the camp in a truck and demanding that the commandant supply him with workers for his munitions factory. Once out of sight of the camp he pulled into the woods and released the inmates. But such audacious acts of defiance were known to the Gestapo, who described Albert's Skoda works in Czechoslovakia as 'a veritable nerve centre for "poor" Czechs', while the Prague police asked for permission to arrest him but were refused.

But by this time Hermann Goering's influence was on the wane and Albert was in hiding after a warrant had been issued for his arrest. Hermann managed to intervene on his brother's behalf by making a personal plea to Himmler, but warned Albert that it would be the last favour he could pull.

CURSED BY THE FAMILY NAME

A year later the brothers were reunited in Augsburg, where Hermann was being held by the Allies, awaiting transfer to Nuremberg, and Albert was being detained on the strength of the Goering name. At this final meeting Hermann hugged him and told him, 'I am very sorry, Albert, that it is you who has to suffer so much for me. You will be free soon. Then take my wife and child under your care. Farewell!'

Ironically it was the Allies who imprisoned Albert for the longest period of his life – two years – and who were unconvinced by his protestations of innocence. While he sat in jail, he compiled a list of 34 prominent people he claimed to have saved and who might be persuaded to speak for him at his trial in Prague. However, he was finally exonerated by the testimony of some of the ordinary Czechs he had rescued from certain death and who wanted it known what he had done.

But the Goering name was a curse from which Albert could not free himself. He declined to change it, even when employers refused to hire him because of its association with the Nazi era and he descended into alcoholism and depression after his Czech wife deserted him, taking their only child to South America.

Albert Goering did not save Jews on the same scale as Oskar Schindler and he may not have been so audacious if he hadn't had his infamous brother to spring him from jail, but there are hundreds of people alive today because of what he did and they don't need reasons or explanations for his behaviour.

Albert Goering is said to have driven up to the Terezin concentration camp and then freed the inmates supplied to him as workers

Reinhard Heydrich

Hitler's Hangman

'I must admit that this gassing had a calming effect on me, I was always horrified at executions by firing squads.'

With his blond hair, blue eyes and Nordic features, SS Obergruppenführer Reinhard Heydrich – Himmler's second-in-command – personified the image of the cold-blooded, clinically efficient Nazi officer; a highly educated and cultured idealist who was caught up in the maelstrom of extreme nationalism and corrupted by a regime that rewarded blind obedience and ruthless efficiency. But an objective assessment of his personality reveals that revenge rather than perverted idealism may account for the zeal with which he organized the most barbaric crimes of the Nazi era.

Many SS leaders, including Himmler and Heydrich, fantasized about belonging to a long line of knights from Germany's mythical past

Heydrich was raised a Catholic in the predominantly Protestant town of Halle, where his father founded a musical conservatory and his mother enjoyed a career as a professional pianist. The family were prosperous, which made Reinhard the envy of his classmates who propagated unsubstantiated rumours that the family had inherited their wealth from Jewish relatives. Heydrich's arrogance and accomplishments, which included proficiency on the violin, only added to their antagonism.

REVILED IN HIS YOUTH

But life at home was not as ideal at it appeared to be. His mother was a strict disciplinarian and beat the boy for any infraction of her rigid rules. School life was equally harsh as classmates ridiculed his thin falsetto voice, while the older boys physically attacked him and taunted him about his reputed Jewish ancestry. He grew up bitter, not with his tormentors – he was too scrawny to fight them – but with the Jews on whom he blamed his troubles. Had he not been ostracized because of his alleged racial origins, he believed he would have been popular and respected. Someone had to pay for his humiliation. He became quiet and withdrawn, putting his energy into athletics and winning several fencing competitions, but his achievements didn't impress his adversaries.

On leaving school Heydrich enlisted in the navy, believing it would bring him the status and respect he felt he was entitled to, but his fellow cadets were equally unforgiving, goading him over his presumed Jewish origins and his love of classical music and taking every opportunity to embarrass and belittle him. They called him 'Billy Goat' because of his high bleating laugh and reviled him for his arrogance and stated ambition to become an admiral.

Despite his unpopularity, Heydrich seemed destined for an illustrious military career until he was court-martialled and dishonourably discharged in the spring of 1931 for breaking off his engagement to his pregnant fiancée, an act 'unbecoming an officer and a gentleman'. He told the tribunal that he refused to marry a woman who had given herself to him so freely. By doing so she had proved herself unsuitable to be the wife of an officer.

FAVOURED BY HIMMLER

As fate would have it, his next romantic entanglement was with a fanatical Nazi, Lina van Osten, who persuaded her future husband to apply to the small but rapidly expanding SS, where his ambition would be recognized and rewarded.

Himmler took an immediate liking to the six foot tall (1.83 m), slender Heydrich who appeared to embody the qualities the Reichsführer valued so highly – namely, thoroughness and the ability to formulate a detailed plan of action from the vaguest idea. At the end of the interview Himmler asked Heydrich to draw up a blueprint for a new security service, the SD (*Sicherheitsdienst*), and was so impressed by the proposal that he hired him immediately. The SD would be independent of the Gestapo and would be charged with investigating those citizens and officials suspected of being disloyal to the Party. It would rely on a network of informers and electronic surveillance, including bugging premises, tapping telephones and using hidden cameras. The organization was to play a crucial role in the discrediting of two top German generals who expressed opposition to Hitler's war plans in 1937. Werner von Blomberg and Werner von Fritsch were framed for crimes they had not committed, giving Hitler reason to dismiss them and assume the role of Commander-in-Chief.

ALLEGATIONS OF JEWISHNESS

Prior to his enlistment, Heydrich had shown little interest in extreme nationalism or the Nazi Party and had been marginalized by his fellow naval officers for his lack of political zeal, but after his appointment he redoubled his efforts to convince his new employer of his commitment to the Nazi cause. And yet rumours of his Jewish ancestry persisted, forcing Himmler to accede to demands for an official investigation, during which Hitler personally interviewed Heydrich in order to reassure himself that the rumours were false. Having satisfied himself, he told Himmler that Heydrich was

'a highly gifted but also very dangerous man, whose gifts the movement had to retain... [Heydrich could be] extremely useful; for he would eternally be grateful to us that we had kept him and not expelled him and would obey blindly.'

Heydrich was appointed Deputy Protector of Bohemia and Moravia and he and his family moved into Prague Castle

WANNSEE MEETING

On 20 January 1942, Reinhard Heydrich, now Obergruppenführer of the Reich Main Security Office (the RSHA) – which commanded the Gestapo, the SS Intelligence Service (SD) and the Criminal Police (KRIPO), as well as the Foreign Intelligence Service – convened a meeting of top Nazi officials in a suburb of Berlin. The setting was a villa overlooking the Grosser Wannsee, a favoured beauty spot for vacationing Berliners.

The stated purpose of the meeting was the planning and implementation of Goering's order of 31 July 1941 for the rounding-up, transportation and extermination of the 11 million Jews in Germany and the occupied territories of the East ('the total solution of the Jewish question'). However, Heydrich used it to establish his authority over the various departments who would be co-ordinating their combined resources in the forthcoming operation. He spoke for an hour, during which he outlined the progress that had been made to date on marginalizing the Jews from German society. Then he moved on to the difficult question of establishing the criteria for determining who would be considered suitable for 'resettlement' and who would be exempt, on the grounds of intermarriage, military service (many Jews had served in the Great War) and continuing usefulness to the state. But the Jews were not the only people deemed unworthy of life. The population of the conquered territories was to be reduced by 30 million through starvation, as food and other vital supplies were to be diverted to Germany.

The proceedings were conducted in a brisk and businesslike fashion, with Heydrich's deputy Adolf Eichmann recording the minutes as if it were a conventional board meeting of I.G. Farben, who would soon be bidding to supply the gas chambers with the lethal pesticide Zyklon B.

LANGUAGE OF DEATH

But Heydrich was shrewd enough to realize that their discussion would have to be documented in coded language, so that their true intentions would be unclear if the war turned against them and they were brought to account for their crimes. So he instructed Eichmann to use euphemistic 'office' language when compiling the report at the end of the day. It was decided that 'evacuation' would be used when extermination was really meant.

Eichmann later recalled,

Heydrich proved to be both conscientious and committed and soon compiled thick files on those of questionable loyalty, which earned him rapid promotion. Within two years he had been promoted to brigadier general and had earned the admiration and respect of Himmler.

In June 1934, just two months after Himmler had been appointed head of the newly formed Gestapo, with Heydrich as his second-in-command, the pair hatched a plot to purge the SA of its leadership and settle old scores with dozens of former enemies within the state.

As Himmler's power grew, so Heydrich's influence increased until he was the second most feared man in the SS.

> *'The gentlemen were standing together, or sitting together and were discussing the subject quite bluntly, quite differently from the language which I had to use later in the record. During the conversation they minced no words about it at all... they spoke about methods of killing, about liquidation, about extermination... After the conference, Heydrich, Müller [General Heinrich Müller, head of the Gestapo] and myself sat cozily around the fireplace. We had drinks. We had brandy. We sang songs. After a while, we got up on chairs and drank a toast. Then we got up on the tables and went round and round. On the chairs. On the tables. Then we sat around peacefully, giving ourselves a rest after so many exhausting hours.'*

Heydrich took particular satisfaction from the idea of employing Jews to police the round-up and ensure the orderly transportation of neighbours, friends and even family members from the ghettos to the extermination camps, where they too would meet their deaths when their usefulness had expired. In deceiving the victims into believing that they were merely being resettled in the East, and making them pay for the privilege, he believed he had proved himself intellectually superior and was therefore finally free of the 'stigma' of being racially inferior to his Aryan comrades.

ASSASSINATION

Hitler rewarded his initiative by appointing Heydrich Deputy Protector of Bohemia and Moravia (the Nazi-renamed former Czechoslovakia), a position Heydrich flaunted by riding in an open-topped Mercedes without an armed escort. He was showing his contempt for a population he believed had been terrorized into submission.

His arrogance proved fatal. He was mortally wounded by two Czech OSS agents on the morning of 27 May 1942. He might have recovered had he allowed Czech surgeons to operate but he distrusted them. By the time his chosen physicians arrived the wound had been infected by fibres from his uniform and the horsehair upholstery of the car. Heydrich died from blood poisoning on 4 June.

REINHARD HEYDRICH

BORN: 7 March, 1904, Halle an der Saale, Saxony-Anhalt, Germany
DIED: 4 June, 1942, Prague, Protectorate of Bohemia and Moravia
NICKNAME: Billy Goat, The Hangman, The Blond Beast, The Butcher of Prague

Family: Father: Richard Bruno Heydrich, opera singer/composer; mother: Elisabeth (née Krantz); siblings: Heinz, Maria; wife: Lina; children: Klaus, Heider, Silke, Marte

Career/life: Joined Maercker's Volunteer Rifles, 1918; member of anti-Semitic federation; joins navy, 1922, discharged 1931 for breaking engagement promise; joins SS, 1931, became chief of intelligence service; rumours of Jewish ancestry quashed; head of SD, 1932; head of Gestapo, 1934; Chief of Security Police and SD, 1939; President of Interpol, 1940; Deputy Reich Protector of the Protectorate of Bohemia and Moravia, 1941; chaired Wannsee Conference, 1942; severely wounded by anti-tank grenade, thrown by Jan Kubišin, in Prague, 1942, later died of injuries

Description: Blond, blue-eyed Aryan ideal, but embarrassed by high-pitched voice; totally ruthless, but squeamish when personally witnessing executions; notorious womanizer before marriage; vain and contemptuous of others' shortcomings; highly intelligent; ambitious, always wanted to lead the pack; avoided publicity, public appearances; sadistic sense of humour; talented violinist; excelled at sports

'I believe that Heydrich was the worst criminal of them all. I myself saw him and he looked with such a glance of hatred that I shall never forget it.' Ewald-Heinrich von Kleist-Schmenzin

REINHARD HEYDRICH DOSSIER

› Heydrich engineered a purge of top-ranking Soviet officers in 1937 by supplying Soviet agents with information that implicated the officers in a planned coup against Stalin. The commander-in-chief of the Red Army and seven leading generals were executed.

› After the Anschluss in March 1938, Heydrich established the Central Office for Jewish Emigration to fleece Austrian Jews of their property and valuables in return for exit visas. When Goering saw the potential for enriching himself, he authorized a branch to be set up in Berlin.

› Heydrich orchestrated the 'spontaneous' protests of Kristallnacht in November 1938 as a reprisal for the assassination of a German diplomat in Paris by a Jewish youth whose deportation to France he had authorized. In covering up for his mistake 1,000 synagogues were burnt to the ground, Jewish shops were vandalized and thousands of Jews were transported to concentration camps.

› Heydrich conceived Operation Himmler (aka Operation Konserve) in 1939 to give Germany an excuse to invade Poland. The SS planted the bodies of murdered concentration camp prisoners at a German radio station at Gleiwitz, dressed in Polish Army uniforms to serve as casualties in the fake 'attack'.

› Following the invasion of Poland, Heydrich formed the SS Einsatzgruppen (Special Action Groups) whose task was to round up and execute leading politicians, the aristocracy, the professional elite and the clergy in the East, as well as members of any group which might pose a threat to the occupying forces and their puppet administration. Leaders of the Einsatzgruppen vied with each other to see how many Jews they could execute in a day. By the end of the war it was estimated that they had murdered a total of 1,300,000.

› Heydrich proposed that Jews in the occupied territories should be rounded up and herded into ghettos until their deportation or liquidation could be arranged. Meanwhile starvation and disease would reduce the numbers that had to be dealt with. By the middle of 1941 half a million had died in Krakow, Warsaw and Lodz.

Enraged, Hitler ordered the execution of every adult male in the villages of Lidice and Ležáky and the destruction of both villages. Eighty-one of Lidice's children were deported to Chelmno extermination camp and the remainder were deported to Germany for adoption by Nazi families. Four pregnant women had their babies aborted at the hospital where Heydrich had died and then they were sent to Ravensbrück concentration camp to die with their families and neighbours. In total, more than 1,300 people were murdered and an estimated 13,000 imprisoned as punishment for Heydrich's death.

Heydrich's assassination had been sanctioned by exiled Czech president Beneš in the hope that German reprisals would rouse the Czech people to open rebellion, but the uprising did not happen and many Czechs felt thousands had been needlessly sacrificed to eliminate one hated Nazi.

LEFT: Heydrich's open-topped Mercedes after the attack; it had been unwise of him to travel around occupied Prague without protection

BELOW: Heydrich has a stretch of Prague riverbank named after him, with his widow and grieving mother in attendance

Josef Goebbels

Spin Doctor to the Third Reich

'We shall go down in history as the greatest statesmen of all time, or as the greatest criminals.'

According to Magda Goebbels' biographer Hans-Otto Meissner, Josef Goebbels had no particular hatred for the Jews – he hated almost everyone. And the feeling was mutual. As a child he was shunned by other children partly because of his physical deformity, but also because he abhorred company.

GETTING HIS OWN BACK

At the age of seven he had been diagnosed with osteomyelitis (inflammation of the bone marrow) and had to have an operation which left him with a club foot and a permanent limp. It also meant he had to wear a brace. He made no effort to befriend other boys and he actively deterred any efforts to include him in social or family activities. He became withdrawn and sarcastic, using his sharp tongue to fend off abuse instead of his fists. Consequently other children, and adults too, kept their distance, leaving the boy more isolated than ever.

As his mother remarked, 'Since he was physically inferior he had to prove to others, as well as to himself, that he was more intelligent. He jumped at the chance to make sport of them, to criticize them, to scorn them.'

It was his nature to blame others for his misfortune – first God, to whom he had prayed for a miracle cure but who had abandoned him, and then his own mother, whose blind faith in Catholicism and the curative power of the saints had proven inadequate when her son needed it.

Feeling betrayed by God and having lost his faith in religion, the young Goebbels retreated inwards, finding strength in his own not inconsiderable intellect and then in the Fatherland.

'I always hoped he would believe in my Catholic God,' his mother said, 'but he simply believed in Germany.'

PUBLIC SPEAKER

It wasn't the people that he put his trust in, but their sacred spirit that he dreamed of tapping into, like the Holy Grail of Arthurian myth. And that spirit he thought he sensed in *völkisch* nationalism and the thrill of public speaking, which he discovered while studying literature and philosophy at Heidelberg University.

From the moment he felt the electrifying power surging through him and heard the applause of the audience he forgot his physical disability for a moment and felt the power of the gods. As he said,

'Success is the important thing... I do not care if I give wonderful, aesthetically elegant speeches, or speak so that women cry. The point of a political speech is to persuade people of what we think right, to... conquer the broad masses. Propaganda should be popular, not intellectually pleasing.'

When war was declared in 1914 Goebbels volunteered, encouraged by his teachers and classmates who were inflamed with patriotic fever, but he knew he would be refused on account of his disability. It was almost as if he needed it to be acknowledged, so that he would have justification for not taking an active part. Instead, he ploughed his energies and gift for public speaking into politics, ranting against the wealthy, but not it appears the Jews. Until he came under Hitler's spell anti-Semitism was not an obsession with Goebbels, who held his Jewish teachers in high regard. He freely admitted that he had learned much from Jewish authors and scientists, although he later allowed his own writings in praise of these men to be added to the pyres of burning books.

He came to believe in only two things – his own greatness and his devout cynicism. Success was not attained through talent or hard work, but sheer willpower and a complete lack of scruples, which saw the strongest and most self-centred survive.

Despite Goebbel's deformity he was a notorious serial seducer who detailed his numerous affairs with young actresses in his voluminous diaries – which totalled 30,000 pages. As the Reich Minister for Public Enlightenment and Propaganda, he commanded the biggest 'casting couch' in Germany, determining which young women were awarded parts in film, theatre and radio, a pursuit which earned him the nickname 'The Ram'.

It was the law of the jungle, the principle of dog eat dog and Goebbels intended to come out on top, deferring only to the even more unscrupulous and pitiless leader of the pack – Hitler. He cynically said,

> *'Man is and remains an animal.*
> *Here a beast of prey, there a house pet,*
> *but always an animal.'*

FINDS HIS RELIGION

The day he witnessed Hitler speak, in June 1922, Goebbels had found his new religion and from that moment he devoted his life to converting others to the cause.

Goebbels at a gymnastic exhibition in Stuttgart, 1933

JOSEF GOEBBELS

BORN: 29 October, 1897, Rheydt, Prussia, Germany

DIED: 1 May, 1945, Berlin, Germany

NICKNAME: The Poison Dwarf, The Ram

Family: Father: Fritz Goebbels, factory clerk; mother: Maria (née Odenhausen; of Dutch descent); siblings: Hans, Konrad, Elisabeth, Maria; wife: Magda; children: Helga, Hildegard, Helmut, Holdine, Hedwig, Heidrun; stepson: Harald (from Magda's previous marriage)

Career/life: PhD, Heidelberg, 1921; failed author/playwright; joined Nazi Party, 1924; summoned by Hitler, 1926, became loyal follower; Party Gauleiter for Berlin, 1926; elected to Reichstag, 1928; organized election campaigns, 1930–33; made Minister of Propaganda, 1933; organized Kristallnacht, 1938; Reich Plenipotentiary for Total War, 1944; arranged cyanide poisoning of own children then committed suicide with Magda

Description: Very short in stature, with deformed right leg; embittered by physique and literary failures; anti-capitalist socialist who forwent principles to follow Hitler; virulent anti-Semite; gifted public speaker; sharp, sarcastic tongue, resulting in nickname; propaganda genius; dictated what form German culture should take; used position to become serial womanizer

'Think of the press as a great keyboard on which the government can play.'

'National Socialism is a religion. All we lack is a religious genius capable of uprooting outmoded religious practices and putting new ones in their place. We lack traditions and ritual. One day soon National Socialism will be the religion of all Germans. My party is my church, and I believe I serve the Lord best if I do his will, and liberate my oppressed people from the fetters of slavery. That is my gospel.'

Anyone who questioned such beliefs or accused the Führer of being a false messiah was dealt with as pitilessly as the Inquisition had silenced those they considered heretics five hundred years before. The New Order threatened to be a new Dark Age, only this time on a far greater scale and with books being consigned to the flames as well as human beings. Ideas that were not consistent with National Socialist ideology were held to be as dangerous as armed resistance. He who proclaimed his beliefs loudest and longest would prevail, whether it was the truth or not. That was the principle behind propaganda and Goebbels was, for a time, the master.

'The most brilliant propagandist technique will yield no success unless one fundamental principle is borne in mind constantly – it must confine itself to a few points and repeat them over and over... It is not propaganda's task to be intelligent, its task is to lead to success.'

RIGHT: Josef and Magda Goebbels on their wedding day in Mecklenburg with her son in Nazi uniform and Hitler behind them

MAGDA GOEBBELS
The Nazis' First Lady

'Love is meant for husbands, but my love for Hitler is stronger, I would give my life for it.'

Magda acted the part of the devoted Nazi mother for the press and newsreel propaganda machine, but behind the scenes she was deeply unhappy and hurt by her husband's numerous affairs. Each time she learned about a new conquest, he would swear that it meant nothing and that she was the only love of his life. But when he fell for Lída Baarová, a glamorous Czech film star, Magda was furious and asked for a private meeting with Hitler, at which she begged the Führer for permission to divorce. But Hitler couldn't risk a scandal and sent for Goebbels. If he

didn't end the affair, Hitler would have him assigned to Japan. A chastened Goebbels returned to his wife and the Czech movie starlet was sent home.

In his memoirs, *Inside the Third Reich*, Albert Speer tells of another time when Magda confronted her husband with the evidence of his latest affair and threatened to leave him for another man. She only relented after suffering one of his infamous outbursts which eventually wore her down.

> 'It was frightful, the way my husband threatened me. I was just beginning to recuperate at Gastein when he turned up at the hotel. For three days he argued with me incessantly until I could no longer stand it. He used the children to blackmail me; he threatened to take them away from me. What could I do? The reconciliation is only for show... I'm so unhappy, but I have no choice.'

FAILED MARRIAGE

She remained for the sake of the children, all of whom were perhaps named in honour of Hitler: Helga, Hildegard, Helmut, Holdine, Hedwig and Heidrun. But the older ones suspected their mother was putting a brave face on for their benefit. She seemed to be spending more time away from them than ever, recovering from another of her periodic heart murmurs or the painful neuralgia attacks which paralyzed one side of her face. When she returned to their estate in Bogensee outside Berlin, the children's nanny, Frau Hübner, recalls Magda moping around the great house like a doomed Wagnerian heroine, accompanied by tragic arias from the phonograph.

When the music stopped there would be hysterical scenes between Magda and her mother, Auguste, who lived in a bungalow on the grounds and was seemingly in a constant state of hysteria, haranguing her daughter for marrying 'that odious man' and threatening to kill herself because no one understood her.

Their paternal grandmother, Katherina, also lived on the estate and every Sunday the children were

Lída Baarová, the glamorous Czech film star Goebbels fell for

brought in to sing to the old woman. Katherina was a formidable personality who believed in speaking her mind no matter how hurtful or embarrassing it might be for others.

Nanny Hübner remembers how Goebbels liked to tease the children in a way that suggested he was testing their affection. There was something cruel about it in her opinion and it might have been in response to the way he was treated by his own mother, who was continually criticizing him and complaining 'What has that boy done now?'

MAGDA GOEBBELS

BORN: 11 November, 1901, Berlin, Germany
DIED: 1 May, 1945, Berlin, Germany

Family: Father: Oskar Ritschel; mother: Auguste (née Behrend); stepfather (after parents' divorce) Richard Friedländer; husbands: Günther Quandt (1921), Josef Goebbels (1931); children: Harald, Helga, Hildegard, Helmut, Holdine, Hedwig, Heidrun

Life: Joined Nazi Party, 1930; became loyal Hitler follower; worked as Goebbels' helper and fulfilled Party wife duties; plagued by Goebbels' many affairs, own affairs rumoured; moved into Führerbunker when Soviets entered Berlin, 1945; arranged deaths of children, then took own life alongside Goebbels

Description: Acknowledged beauty; accustomed to wealth, upper-class bearing, seen by Nazis as 'First Lady of Third Reich'; Goebbels originally smitten by her, perhaps Hitler also; often ill and bed-ridden in later war years

'We will take them [the children] *with us, because they are too good, too lovely for the world which lies ahead.'*

CHILDREN OF THE NAZIS

According to Frau Hübner, Goebbels had a strained relationship with his children. He once wrote in his diary, 'I speak to the children on the telephone. They are all so sweet. How attached one can become to such tiny, insignificant beings!'

He had no reservations about using his own children for propaganda purposes. In 1944 he had Helga and Hildegard visit a military hospital to boost morale, but had to abandon plans to include it in a newsreel when the girls became traumatized by the sight of so many severely disfigured patients.

The children were frequently photographed with their 'Uncle' Adolf, sharing chocolate cake at the Berghof and accompanying him on outings to the countryside and the sea.

Helga had been Hitler's favourite, but she was reluctant to be left in his company as is evident in a photograph taken when she was three. She stares fiercely at the camera with her back to him, her legs crossed, and there is no sign of affection or closeness from either of them.

UNITED IN DEATH

'The impacts are shaking the bunker. The elder kids cover the younger ones, their presence is a blessing and they are making the Führer smile once in a while. May God help that I have the strength to perform the last and hardest. We only have one goal left: loyalty to the Führer even in death.'

There is something disturbing about the formal family portrait of a mother and her six immaculately groomed children posing with the father and his stepson in a photographer's studio sometime in 1942 (though the stepson's image was added later).

Although all of the children are smiling and their mother is too, we are now aware that this was the last family photograph, because the mother killed herself and her children three years after this picture

The perfect Nazi family?: Magda and Josef Goebbels with Helga, Hildegard, Helmut, Hedwig, Holdine, Heidrun and Harald (added later)

UNCLE ADOLF

› As the battle for Berlin raged above them the Goebbels children played with other Nazi offspring. Hitler would occasionally drink cocoa with them and he allowed them to use his bathtub.

› After a failed attempt to poison him in 1933, Hitler asked Magda to prepare all his meals.

› Magda asked Hitler for permission to divorce Goebbels after she discovered that he had been having an affair with a famous Czech actress, but Hitler persuaded them to be reconciled and threatened Goebbels with a foreign posting if he strayed again.

› Magda's only surviving child from her first marriage was her stepson Harald, a Luftwaffe pilot, whose father was the wealthy industrialist Günther Quandt.

› Harald was killed in an air crash in 1967, aged 45. His four daughters are now billionaires thanks to prudent investments made by their grandfather Günther, Magda's first husband.

› In her final letter to Harald, written from the Goebbels family's quarters in the Führerbunker, she assured him that her National Socialist ardour had not diminished. 'Our glorious idea is ruined and with it everything beautiful and marvellous that I have known in my life. The world that comes after the Führer and national socialism is not any longer worth living in and therefore I took the children with me, for they are too good for the life that would follow... May God help that I have the strength to perform the last and hardest. We only have one goal left: loyalty to the Führer even in death.'

› Magda trained as a Red Cross nurse during the war and worked at the electronics factory Telefunken, travelling to work each day on the bus.

was taken. She didn't commit this most heinous act because she was homicidal, but simply because she had been indoctrinated by her husband, Josef Goebbels, to believe that they were too good to live in a world without their Führer, Adolf Hitler. It is one of countless crimes committed in the name of the Third Reich, but it is the one which illustrates perhaps more than any other the degree of control it exerted over those it had brainwashed into believing its own propaganda.

Magda Goebbels was not an unintelligent woman, nor was she weak and impressionable, but it would have taken an extraordinary woman to resist her husband's persuasive powers and in those last days in the Berlin bunker Magda's willpower had been worn down to the bone. She was suffering from depression and was physically exhausted from the effects of a heart condition and a severe attack of neuralgia. But she could have tolerated her ailments and remained with her children on their estate outside Berlin had it not been for the sense of duty that drew her to the besieged Führerbunker.

She told her sister-in-law, Eleanore (Ello) Quandt, 'We have demanded monstrous things from the German people, treated other nations with pitiless cruelty. For this the victors will exact their full revenge... we can't let them think we are cowards. Everybody else has the right to live. We haven't got this right – we have forfeited it.'

Ello attempted to reassure her that she was not responsible for crimes committed by her husband, but Magda disagreed.

> 'I make myself responsible. I belonged. I believed in Hitler and for long enough in Josef Goebbels... Suppose I remain alive? I should immediately be arrested and interrogated about Josef. If I tell the truth I must reveal what sort of man he was – must describe all that happened behind the scenes. Then any respectable person would turn from me in disgust.'

Faced with the choice of death or defending Goebbels, she assured her sister-in-law that to defend him would be to go against her conscience. She couldn't live with the knowledge of what he had done and if she was to die, then the children must die too.

> 'We will take them with us, they are too good, too lovely for the world which lies ahead. In the days to come Josef will be regarded as one of the greatest criminals that Germany has ever produced. His children would hear that said daily, people would torment them, despise and humiliate them.... You know how I told you at the time quite frankly what the Führer said in the Cafe Anast in Munich when he saw the little Jewish boy, you remember? That he would like to squash him flat like a bug on the wall... I couldn't believe it and thought it was just provocative talk. But he really did it later. It was all so unspeakably gruesome.'

Like a member of a religious cult, she had been conditioned to see their leader as a messiah who was being persecuted by a hostile world. And a world without their saviour was not a world they wished to live in.

Even Hitler had initially urged Magda to save herself and the children, but when he saw that she was determined to die by her husband's side, he conceded that it was best that the children were not allowed to live without their parents. It was this tacit approval that Magda used to force one of the bunker's inhabitants, Dr Helmut Kunz, to administer the morphine injections that would put the children to sleep before she fed each of them a poison capsule. Kunz later testified to having refused her three times, but Magda threatened to have him shot if he didn't

assist her. It was the last act of a devoted mother, as she saw it, and it took her last ounce of strength to see it through. Bruising on the arms of the eldest daughter suggests that she had to be restrained while her mother forced the cyanide between her lips. Afterwards Magda emerged from the room tearful but stoic.

She said nothing but sat down with a pack of cards and began silently playing patience. (A witness claimed Hitler's physician Dr Stumpfegger had given the children a drugged drink, but Dr Kunz confessed after the war and was tried for being an accessory to the crime.)

It was 1 May 1945, the day after Hitler's suicide. Some hours later she and her husband would climb the stairs to the Reich Chancellery garden, where Goebbels shot her in the back of the head before killing himself. (Other sources claim both were shot by the SS after taking cyanide.) Their bodies were soaked in petrol and set alight but only partially burned.

After the Russians had stormed the bunker they transported the bodies of the Goebbels family to Magdeburg, where they remained for 25 years. They were then exhumed, cremated and crushed before the ashes were thrown into the river.

Amon Goeth

The Nazi Butcher

'When you saw Goeth, you saw death.'

Poldek Pfefferberg

Many of the Nazi hierarchy committed their crimes from behind a desk. Very few of the leadership bloodied their own hands. But Amon Goeth enjoyed killing and as commandant of the Krakow-Plaszów forced labour camp in Poland he had a licence to kill with impunity.

MURDER FOR PLEASURE

An early convert to the Nazi cause, Austrian-born Goeth rose in the ranks of the SS until he was assigned to Operation Reinhard in the summer of 1942 and given responsibility for rounding up and transporting Jews to the extermination camps at Treblinka, Belzec and Sobibor. For his efficiency and unstinting dedication he was appointed commandant of the newly constructed Krakow-Plaszów labour camp in the spring of 1943, which was populated with the survivors of the liquidated Krakow ghetto.

Until the camp was upgraded to a concentration camp and staffed by the SS, Goeth was permitted to do as he wished, which meant indulging his mania for dispensing death like a depraved despot. His favourite amusement was picking off prisoners at random with a high-powered rifle from the upper window of his villa, which overlooked the compound, but he also got a special thrill from setting his two vicious dogs on prisoners indiscriminately and watching as they tried in vain to fend them off. When he finally called off his dogs he looked down at the lifeless bloodied flesh with a smirk that betrayed a pride in his well-trained pets, as if they had dragged in a slaughtered rabbit for their master's approval.

SADISTIC KILLER

Goeth was a textbook psychopath who relished the power over life and death that his post had given him. But he didn't merely murder those who stood helpless before him, he took a sadistic delight in their suffering.

A Polish prisoner, Wladyslaw Kopystecki, testified that he personally witnessed Goeth shoot a starving female prisoner found eating a potato in the kitchen. Goeth then ordered her to be thrown into a cauldron of boiling water while evidently still alive. When he saw that she was thrashing about, he ordered other inmates to cover the pot and then walked away as if nothing untoward had occurred.

A 'consignment' of Jewish women and girls from one of the Polish ghettos at a 'reloading point' near Warsaw in 1944

AMON GOETH

BORN: 11 December, 1908, Vienna, Austria
DIED: 13 September, 1946, Kraków, Poland
NICKNAME: The Nazi Butcher

Family: Goeth's parents were in the 'book publishing industry' – little else appears to be known about them; wives: Olga (née Janauschek), Anny (née Geiger); children: Peter (died in infancy), Werner, Ingeborg (all by Anny); Monika (by Ruth Kalder, his mistress)

Career/life: Joined Nazi youth group, 1925, then anti-Semitic Heimwehr, 1927–30; joined Nazi Party, 1930, Austrian SS the same year; worked for exiled Austrian Nazi Party in Munich, 1933, supplying arms, munitions to Austrian Nazis; arrested and escaped, worked with parents until 1937; resumed Party activities, 1938; part of Operation Reinhard, 1942, codename for extermination of Polish Jews; given command of Płaszów camp, 1943, and liquidation of Tarnów ghetto and Szebnie camp; arrested by SS, 1944, for his activities, committed to mental institution, where he was arrested by the US; tried and sentenced to death in Poland

Description: Tall (6 ft 4 in [1.93 m]), heavy set, blue eyes, wore a white shirt or a black leather coat and high boots; carried a rifle, his two dogs at his heels; sometimes pictured in full Nazi uniform on a white horse or bare-chested on his balcony, again holding a rifle; prisoners were killed or beaten by him for the smallest 'offence', or he set his dogs on them; took delight in taunting and torturing inmates

'One day he hanged a friend of mine just because he had once been rich. He was the devil.' Anna Duklauer Perl

Escape attempts were punished by summary execution. In the event that a prisoner succeeded, members of their work detail would be shot arbitrarily by Goeth until he had vented his rage. But even minor infractions of the rules were dealt with unmercifully.

He shot his own batman because the man had saddled the wrong horse for his morning ride and he shot one of his two Jewish maids because he was embarrassed at having flirted with her the night before while drunk. He killed others for displeasing him – for meeting his gaze when they should have been looking down to show true deference, for serving his soup too hot or for failing to scrub a ring of grime from his bathtub.

As one of his two Jewish maids later testified, 'Never would I, never, believe that any human being would be capable of such horror, of such atrocities.'

KILLINGS WITHOUT REASON

When the camp was upgraded and the SS installed to take over its management, Goeth continued to dispense death on a whim. On Yom Kippur, 1943, the holiest day in the Jewish calendar, Goeth ordered 50 inmates to be taken out and shot. No reason was given.

His sadism seemed to know no limits. No justification was needed if Goeth got it into his mind that fun could be had from humiliating his victims. He took particular pleasure from tormenting them – forcing them to thank him after they were beaten, restarting the beating if they begged for mercy and making them believe they were safe before he murdered them.

On one occasion, Goeth saw a six-year-old boy scrambling from the back of a truck and assumed he had been hiding something. He called to the boy, 'Come, come, don't be afraid!' The boy stopped to empty his pockets of some toys and trinkets thinking that he would be allowed to go. Goeth took the toys, smiled reassuringly then shot the child dead.

Moshe Bejski – a Schindler Jew who survived to become an Israeli High Court judge – recalled the day

Goeth refused to spare a 15-year-old boy by the name of Haubenstock, whose only crime had been to sing a Russian song.

> 'The boy was hanged and something happened which occurs once in many thousands of cases – the rope broke. The boy stood there, he was again lifted on to a high chair which was placed under the rope, and he began to beg for mercy. An order was given to hang him a second time. And then he was raised a second time to the gallows, and hanged, and thereafter that same Amon Goeth, with his own hands, also fired a shot.'

MENTALLY ILL

Goeth had assembled 15,000 prisoners to witness the execution, so he clearly had no expectation of escaping justice when the war was over. Eventually his superiors turned against him when they discovered he had been hoarding valuables stolen from the inmates, valuables to which the state had prior claim. In September 1944 he was charged with depriving prisoners of adequate food, as well as various infractions of the regulations governing the administration of the camp and the treatment of prisoners, and was subjected to a mental health examination by SS doctors. They determined that he was mentally ill and ordered him to be confined to an asylum, where he was arrested by the Allies after Germany's capitulation. He was tried by the new Polish authorities and hanged for war crimes not far from the Krakow camp.

Monument to the victims of the Nazis at the Krakow-Plaszów camp.

Heinrich Himmler

Puny Exponent of the Master Race

'We have only one task, to stand firm and carry on the racial struggle without mercy.'

Appearances can be deceptive. It was certainly true in the case of Heinrich Himmler, the physically unprepossessing leader of the SS and head of the Gestapo, whose puny physique, poor eyesight and weak constitution would have prohibited him from being accepted into the ranks of the elite military units that he commanded. With his round rimless spectacles, dogmatic manner and obsession with herbal remedies and astrology, he gave the impression of being what Albert Speer called 'half schoolmaster, half crank'.

NAME INSTILLED TERROR

There was nothing remarkable in his appearance or manner which could be considered intimidating, and yet the mere mention of his name was sufficient to instil terror and immediate compliance, not for any qualities that he possessed, but for the unquestioning loyalty that he commanded from those who ruthlessly enforced his orders. His unremarkable appearance and unimposing presence made Himmler an unlikely addition to the rogues' gallery of Nazi war criminals and yet, as Reichsführer-SS and head of the State Secret Police, he was indirectly responsible for authorizing an estimated 14 million civilian deaths in forced labour and extermination camps. And this did not include the countless thousands of unarmed POWs and resistance members murdered by the SS and the Gestapo, the hundreds of thousands liquidated by the Einsatzgruppen death squads in the conquered countries and the unknown number of civilians who were executed in reprisals for alleged acts of sabotage, or for having harboured enemy soldiers.

It was indicative of the regime that its most powerful and feared figure, second only to Hitler himself, was

a man of no discernible qualities or character, other than a talent for intrigue, opportunism and the ability to delegate responsibility to others for organizing mass murder on a scale unparalleled in modern times.

HARSH CHILDHOOD

The second of three sons born to a pedantic Munich high school teacher, Himmler was hampered by an inability to make friends and form relationships which left him isolated and distrustful. A classmate recalled him as having a 'half-malicious, half-embarrassed smile on his face', which didn't endear him to the other pupils, while those who met him in later life also spoke of his fixed, contemptuous or faintly mocking smile. Himmler's steely grey-blue eyes would fix on anyone that he considered his inferior as if probing for signs that betrayed their true intentions. It was imperative for him to know whether or not they could be trusted.

His cold-blooded and suspicious nature had been fostered by his authoritarian and pedantic father, Gebhard, who had been described by a former pupil as the kind of man who 'grovels to his superiors while oppressing his inferiors' and was not above publicly humiliating a pupil he took a dislike to.

Holidays offered his sons no respite from their father's unrelenting schooling which demanded that young Heinrich keep a diary of his activities, a diary that was checked and corrected on a daily basis. It was this strict, inflexible adherence to regulations and the relentless drilling that promoted industry for its own sake that instilled in Himmler an unquestioning obedience to authority and the craving to exercise that degree of authority over others.

UNDER HITLER'S SPELL

There was only one person he deferred to – Adolf Hitler. When he attended a political meeting in a Munich beer keller in 1923 he knew he had found a cause and was soon extolling the virtues of a man he believed to be the future saviour of Germany. Himmler was in awe of Hitler and believed him to be as significant a figure as Jesus Christ. He became a zealot and told anyone who would listen, 'A figure of the greatest brilliance has become incarnate in his person.'

None of the Party leaders gave the wiry, bespectacled youth a second look, but Hitler had an instinct for those who might be useful to him and by 1929 he had made Himmler the head of his private bodyguard, the SS.

ABSOLUTE POWER

The SS had been formed in 1922 to provide a 300-strong Praetorian guard for the Führer, but after Himmler assumed command in 1929 he enlarged it to a force of more than 50,000 men, a force that rivalled the *Sturmabteilung* (SA). The brownshirted stormtroopers of the SA had become all but unmanageable under the leadership of Ernst Roehm and its power threatened the German Army itself.

Himmler, however, could be relied upon to enforce the Führer's will and his men were trained to obey without

Adolf Hitler with Heinrich Himmler in Nuremberg in 1938: Hitler was the only person Himmler deferred to

question. So to appease the German High Command Hitler ordered a purge. He entrusted the SS with rounding up and executing hundreds of high-ranking leaders of the SA and other 'dissident' elements on the Night of the Long Knives in June 1934, not to mention those individuals who were in Hitler's way. Himmler and other Nazi leaders also took the opportunity to settle personal scores. For their loyalty, the SS were rewarded with unparalleled powers, giving them absolute authority over every branch of the German armed forces and the civil authorities. From that day, Himmler and his SS answered to no one but Hitler.

CONCENTRATION CAMP ROLE

If Hitler had failed to amass public support in the critical federal election of 1930 – which saw the NSDAP become the second largest party in the Reichstag – Himmler might have been a chicken farmer. His marriage three years earlier to Margarete Boden, the 34-year-old owner of a private nursing home, had furnished him with the means to buy a small poultry farm after he had persuaded his wife to sell her business and invest in the joint venture. But the unpopularity of the Weimar government and the threat of a communist revolution persuaded many voters to put their faith in the extreme nationalists. And once Hitler was established in the German parliament he found a post worthy of his 'loyal Heinrich'.

Having promoted Himmler to Reichsführer-SS the year before, Hitler now entrusted him with organizing the internment of the Party's political enemies, undesirables and *Untermenschen* – the 'subhumans' whose fate would ultimately be determined by a man obsessed with the myth of Aryan superiority and the subjugation of 'inferior' races.

Given full authority to treat the inmates as he saw fit, Himmler was free to work them to death after selecting the fitter specimens for the slave worker programmes at Peenemünde and other research establishments, or to sign them over to the medical division at Dachau as subjects in sadistic experiments. Himmler saw himself as a patron of science – but it was barbaric and perverted science, which deliberately subjected prisoners to spurious tests and unnecessary surgical operations that were really no more than acts of torture.

Himmler (far left) with his indulgent mother, demanding headmaster father, two brothers and maid

HEINRICH HIMMLER

BORN: 7 October, 1900, Munich, Bavaria
DIED: 23 May, 1945, Lüneburg, Lower Saxony, Germany
NICKNAME: The Faithful Heinrich

Family: Father: Gebhard Himmler, teacher; mother: Anna (née Heyder); siblings: Gebhard, Ernst; wife: Margarete; children: Gudrun (by Margarete), Helge, Nanette (by Hedwig Potthast); foster child: Gerhard, son of a deceased SS officer

Career/life: First World War ended before he finished officer training; studied agriculture, then took office job; joined Nazi Party, 1923, involved in Munich Putsch; joined SS, 1925, took over in 1929 – SS had 52,000 members by 1933, all 'good Aryan types'; set up first concentration camp, Dachau, 1933; took control of Gestapo, 1934; his SS played major part in Night of the Long Knives, 1934, making SS all-powerful; Chief of German Police, 1936, including Gestapo; formed military SS branch, which became the Waffen-SS; Reich Commissar for the Strengthening of Germandom, 1939; when put in charge of German forces facing the US, then Russia, in 1944, he became aware of Germany's weak position and sought peace with the Allies; Hitler ordered his arrest but he escaped into the arms of the Allies in 1945; he swallowed a cyanide capsule before being interrogated

Description: Small, insignificant-looking, receding chin, grey eyes looking through thick pince-nez glasses, mousy moustache, quiet demeanour, smiled a lot, over-courteous

'The best political weapon is the weapon of terror. Cruelty commands respect.'

ELITE BROTHERHOOD

The man described by German historian Joachim Fest as 'the most dreadful combination of... quack and inquisitor that history has ever known' revealed his psychosis in a speech to SS Group Leaders on 4 October 1943:

'One principle must be absolute for the SS man: we must be honest, decent, loyal, and comradely to members of our own blood and to no one else. What happens to the Russians, what happens to the Czechs, is a matter of utter indifference to me. Such good blood of our own kind as there may be among the nations we shall acquire for ourselves, if necessary by taking away the children and bringing them up among us. Whether the other peoples live in comfort or perish of hunger interests me only in so far as we need them as slaves for our culture; apart from that it does not interest me... We Germans, who are the only people in the world who have a decent attitude to animals, will also adopt a decent attitude to these human animals, but it is a crime against our own blood to worry about them and to bring them ideals.'

In Himmler's mind the SS were a black-uniformed brotherhood on whom he could project his distorted romantic ideals, but to whom he could never belong. Instead he exercised a strict paternal interest in the moral welfare of his men, testing their loyalty and fanaticism as rigorously as he evaluated their physical strength and their courage under fire. He saw himself primarily as an educator, but according to one biographer exhibited an 'obsession with interfering in other people's private affairs and [an] almost voyeuristic interest in collecting details about their lives'. Under Himmler's patronage, the SS came to see themselves as an elite to whom the normal rules and regulations of warfare did not apply, a belief enforced by the fact that they were exempt from prosecution in the civil and military courts.

CREATING A MASTER RACE

On 12 December 1935 Himmler established the *Lebensborn* programme, which paired his men with 'racially pure' partners (most of them unmarried) to produce perfect Aryan babies. The aim was to counter Germany's declining birth rate and swell the ranks of the SS and later to offset the casualties at the front. The 21 *Lebensborn* homes were decorated with furniture and fittings stolen from the homes of wealthy Jews, a process presided over personally by the Reichsführer, who also took it upon himself to screen suitable female partners. He is also known to have taken a personal interest in children born on his birthday, sending them gifts and keeping a keen eye on their progress.

But the programme didn't produce enough children to meet Himmler's target, so in 1939 he gave orders for the SS to kidnap 'racially good' children from the Eastern occupied territories. Many were orphans, but thousands were taken forcibly from their parents and subjected to Germanization, conditioning and indoctrination. It is estimated that 100,000 children were stolen from Poland alone. Those who resisted were beaten or transported to the death camps.

KNIGHTS OF THE ROUND TABLE

Himmler demanded the highest standards of conduct from men who would be branded as criminals when the SS was declared illegal after the war, threatening the severest punishment for any man who stole so much as a cigarette from one of their countless victims. As head of both the SS and the Gestapo, he authorized some of the worst atrocities in history – yet he had almost fainted at the sight of a mass execution in Minsk in 1941 and thought nothing of ordering the murder of civilians while scolding his doctor for hunting defenceless animals.

'How can you find pleasure, Herr Kersten, in shooting from behind cover at poor creatures browsing on the edge of a wood, innocent, defenceless and unsuspecting? It's really pure murder. Nature is so marvellously beautiful and every animal has a right to live.'

The *Lebensborn* (Fount of Life) project was set up to produce Aryan babies without taking account of the needs of anyone involved

HIMMLER DOSSIER

› He acquired his obsession with homeopathy, herbalism and astrology from his wife, Margarete Boden, who had served as a nurse in the war and later owned a private nursing home.

› Himmler's godfather was Prince Heinrich of Bavaria, whom his father had tutored. Himmler was brought up to have the manners and skills of a court servant.

› His interest in the healing properties of herbs prompted him to order the planting of herb gardens in the concentration camps.

› Himmler was probably the only SS officer not to see action. He had enlisted in the First World War, but too late to be sent to the front.

› In his early years he worked as a salesman for a fertilizer manufacturer and ran a poultry farm.

› Himmler used to impersonate Hitler when telling others what the Führer had told him.

› He believed himself to be the reincarnation of Heinrich the Fowler, a first-century German king who had subdued the Slavs.

However, human beings, defenceless or otherwise, did not merit such consideration when they offended his superior Aryan sensibilities. Their eradication was of no concern if it enabled the master race to assert its rightful place in the human hierarchy by establishing a new feudal order in Europe, enforced by his black-uniformed Teutonic knights.

In this Wagnerian fantasy, Himmler imagined himself presiding over a kingdom of contented peasants tilling the land while slave workers laboured at heavy industry under the lash of their new masters. He would be enthroned in his lavishly refurbished medieval fortress at Wewelsburg, Westphalia. The castle had been chosen by the Reichsführer-SS for its mystical location. It was believed to have been built on a site where natural power lines of earth energy converged, making it an impenetrable outpost for the final apocalyptic battle with the barbarians from the East, which had been predicted by his personal astrologer and occult advisers. At Wewelsburg, the remains of fallen SS heroes were interred in the stone vault beneath the Great Hall while their comrades communed with their spirits, seated in eerie silence around a magnificent oak table like the knights of Arthurian legend.

FINAL BETRAYAL

An indication of how removed from reality Himmler had become by the end of the war can be determined from the greeting he gave to a representative of the World Jewish Congress, who came to discuss surrender terms on 21 April 1945.

'Welcome to Germany, Herr Masur. It is time you Jews and we National Socialists buried the hatchet.' And on 1 May he met with Admiral Doenitz, who had been appointed Führer after Hitler's death, and spoke of his own 'widespread reputation' abroad, as if it was a reputation to be proud of.

Shortly afterwards, when SS officers learned of his attempts to make a separate peace with the Allies and of Hitler's anger at his betrayal, many committed suicide, feeling that they too had been betrayed by the man who had sworn them to an oath of loyalty.

In the end, Himmler's arrogance proved his undoing. He attempted to escape by disguising himself as a sergeant-major in the Secret Military Police, a branch of the Gestapo, which qualified him for certain arrest. After being captured by the British at Lüneburg on 23 May 1945, he foolishly ordered his fellow POWs to do his chores for him, which prompted one of them to inform the guards. His identity discovered, Himmler swallowed cyanide and was dead within seconds. There was no alternative for a man who knew he would be forced to face the enormity of his crimes in the glare of a public courtroom. And worse – confront himself.

Himmler leads a service at Quedlinburg in honour of Heinrich the Fowler – Reinhard Heydrich is one of the officers behind him

Rudolf Hoess

The Devoted Father Who Murdered Children

'It is tragic that, although I was by nature gentle, good-natured, and very helpful, I became the greatest destroyer of human beings who carried out every order to exterminate people no matter what.'

Behind the metal gate the children played in the garden, squealing with delight as they rode their pedal cars on the paved paths around the flowerbeds. There were five: Klaus, his younger brother Hans-Rudolf, their two sisters Ingebrigitt and Heidetraut and the baby, Annegret, cradled in her mother's arms.

SEPARATING HOME AND WORK

It was an idyllic life. The house was a miniature villa in the Bavarian style, there were maids to tidy up their toys and every evening their father came home from work to sit with them at the dinner table, to play hide-and-seek, to read to them and tuck them into bed at night. There was only one time they could remember him being angry with them and they still didn't fully

Deportation of Jews from the Lodz ghetto to Auschwitz, July 1944

understand why. Their Polish maid Janina had sewn patches on their clothes and made an armband with the word 'capo' (trustee) on it for the older boy, after they had asked her to make them cloth 'badges' like the 'others' wore so they could play 'us' and 'them'. But when their father saw them, he flew into a rage, ushered them inside and tore off the armband and badges.

Every morning 'papa' would button up his tunic, straighten his cap and kiss their mother before going off to work. There were only two rules he insisted upon. No one talked about his work – they only knew that it was a job requiring great responsibility and that it was 'important' – and none of the children were permitted to go beyond the gate. However, Klaus was old enough to guess what was going on. From an upper window he could see the chimneys that rose into the sky on the other side of the high wall surrounding their garden and he knew what the black ash was that spewed from those chimneys. He didn't say anything, but when his mother said they should wash the 'dust' from their freshly picked strawberries before they ate them, he made sure his younger brothers and sisters did as they were told.

PROUD BOAST

Rudolf Hoess was personally responsible for the deaths of an estimated 2.5 million people at Auschwitz, the extermination camp in Galicia, Poland, that he had been given command of in 1940 after he had proved his usefulness and efficiency, first at Dachau and then at Sachsenhausen.

He proudly boasted that he could 'get rid of 10,000 people in 24 hours' and saw nothing criminal in supervising the most notorious of the Nazi death factories, where the sadistic Dr Mengele carried out his perverse medical experiments on living prisoners, many of them women and children. Hoess excused his actions by reminding himself that the victims had already been condemned to death by the Gestapo. From time to time the dreaded secret police would send consignments of condemned prisoners to be killed by lethal injections of benzene, which the camp doctors administered as casually as if they were conventional inoculations.

CHILDREN KILLED FIRST

Hoess also oversaw the actions of subordinates such as Wilhelm Boger, who was seen torturing inmates by beating their genitals until they lost consciousness or died as they lay naked on a metal contraption of his own devising. Sometimes the SS guards didn't wait to

RUDOLF HOESS

BORN: 25 November, 1900, Baden-Baden, Germany
DIED: 16 April, 1947, Auschwitz, Poland
NICKNAME: The Death Dealer of Auschwitz

Family: He came from a strict Catholic family; father: Franz Hoess, shopkeeper; mother: Lina (née Speck); siblings: two unidentified younger sisters; wife: Hedwig; children: Ingebrigitt, Klaus, Hans-Rudolf, Heidetraut, Annegret

Career/life: Joined German Army aged 14; made youngest NCO at 17, heavily decorated; renounced Catholicism, joined Nazi Party, 1922; jailed for murder, 1923, released 1928; joined SS, 1934, assigned to Dachau; joined Waffen-SS, 1938; appointed commandant of Auschwitz, 1940, began exterminating Jews 1941; became chief inspector of camps in 1943; hid under assumed name when Red Army neared, 1946; his wife gave his location away, under pressure, to protect her son, and he was arrested by the Allies; tried and sentenced in Poland and hanged at Auschwitz in 1947

Description: Mild-mannered family man who adored his own children and was kind to animals; originally a Catholic, like his father, but renounced faith; proud of his 'efficient' extermination methods; exaggerated sense of duty, would do whatever was asked of him; always calm and collected, seemed unable to recognize enormity of his crimes

'It was certainly an extraordinary and monstrous order. Nevertheless the reasons behind the extermination programme seemed to me right.'

process the victims, but killed them indiscriminately.

Boger was seen by another observer beating a little boy to death by banging his head repeatedly against a brick wall, then casually eating the apple the child had been holding only moments before. Hoess was not ignorant of such horrors, as he coolly admitted on the stand at Nuremberg.

> 'Children of tender years were invariably exterminated since by reason of their youth they were unable to work... we endeavoured to fool the victims into thinking that they were to go through a delousing process. Of course, frequently they realized our true intentions and we sometimes had riots and difficulties due to that fact. Very frequently women would hide their children under their clothes, but of course when we found them we would send the children in to be exterminated. We were required to carry out these exterminations in secrecy but of course the foul and nauseating stench from the continuous burning of bodies permeated the entire area and all of the people living in the surrounding communities knew that exterminations were going on at Auschwitz.'

Everyone it seems but his own children, for whom he wrote poems, one of which was entitled 'The Beauty of Auschwitz'.

CHOOSING THE BEST METHOD

Hoess placed great faith in duty, which had been instilled in him from an early age by his father, a pious Catholic shopkeeper who had served as an army officer in German East Africa and who had wanted his son to become a priest.

So when his superior, SS Reichsführer Heinrich Himmler, ordered Hoess to initiate the liquidation of the prisoners in 1941 he obeyed. The order had come from the highest authority and it was not for him to question it.

Hitler had given orders 'for the Final Solution of the Jewish question' and had 'chosen the Auschwitz camp for this purpose'. It was more than duty, it was an honour.

> 'The "Final Solution" of the Jewish question meant the complete extermination of all Jews in Europe. I was ordered to establish extermination facilities at Auschwitz in 6/1941... I visited Treblinka to find out how they carried out their exterminations. The camp commandant at Treblinka told me that he had liquidated 80,000 in the course of one half year... He used monoxide gas, and I did not think that his methods were very efficient. So when I set up the extermination building at Auschwitz, I used Zyklon B, which was a crystallized prussic acid which we dropped into the death chamber from a small opening. It took from 3–15 minutes to kill the people in the death chamber, depending upon climatic conditions. We knew when the people were dead because their screaming stopped. We usually waited about one-half hour before we opened the doors and removed the bodies. After the bodies were removed our special Kommandos took off the rings and extracted the gold from the teeth of the corpses.
>
> 'Another improvement we made over Treblinka was that we built our gas chamber to accommodate 2,000 people at one time, whereas at Treblinka their 10 gas chambers only accommodated 200 people each.'

Hoess took a keen personal interest in the process, observing the effects to satisfy his own curiosity.

> 'The gassing was carried out in the detention cells of Block 11. Protected by a gas mask, I watched the killing myself. In the crowded cells, death came instantaneously the moment the Zyklon B was thrown in. A short, almost smothered cry, and it was all over... I must even admit that this gassing set my mind at rest, for the mass extermination of the Jews was to start soon, and at that time neither Eichmann nor I was certain as to how these mass killings were to be carried out. It would be by gas, but we did not know which gas and how it was to be used. Now we had the gas, and we had established a procedure.'

The interior of the gas chamber at Auschwitz II, Birkenau which was described by the Nazis to victims as the 'shower room'

DEDICATION TO DUTY

In 1943 Hoess was rewarded for his dedication by being appointed chief inspector of the camps in Poland and was praised for being a 'true pioneer' in an SS report which commended him for his 'new ideas and educational methods'.

He admitted to only one failing, his reluctance to force screaming children into the gas chambers while they begged for their lives.

'I did, however, always feel ashamed of this weakness of mine after I talked to Adolf Eichmann. He explained to me that it was especially the children who have to be killed first, because where was the logic in killing a generation of older people and leaving alive a generation of young people who can be possible avengers of their parents and can constitute a new biological cell for the re-emerging of this people?'

After his capture he was interviewed by a Polish psychiatrist, Professor Batawia, who observed that Hoess's childhood was...

'stamped with principles of military discipline and religious fanaticism, accompanied by constant emphasis of sin and guilt and the need to do penance. Hoess grew up in a family atmosphere in which expressions of love, freedom from worry, spontaneity, and humour were paralyzed; where everything the child did was judged by strict moral standards, where the word "duty" had almost mystical significance and disobedience in trifles was almost a crime.'

Nazi ideology became Hoess's new religion and he considered it a mortal sin to question an order. In his prison memoirs he claimed that his greatest fear was that any lack of resolve on his part would be seen as cowardice, unworthy of a member of the Aryan Master Race, so he cultivated an attitude of icy indifference. He had nothing personally against the Jews, he declared, but duty demanded that he should obey without recourse to his own conscience.

After being found guilty, Hoess was taken back to Auschwitz in April 1947 and hanged on a specially erected gallows within sight of the villa he had shared with his family.

Josef Mengele

The Angle of Death

'It would be a sin, a crime... and irresponsible not to utilize the possibilities that Auschwitz had for twin research [...] there would never be another chance like it.'

The children were screaming. They didn't know if they would ever see their parents again. Many were too young to know where they were or what was happening to them. The shouting of the men at the ramp had frightened them as they were herded off the cattle wagons, but after they were told that they didn't have to have their hair cut off like the other children and would be allowed to keep their own clothes they stopped crying. They must have thought they were going to a new kindergarten when they were told they had been singled out for 'special treatment' and were ordered to line up. And once they had been shepherded into special barracks by the *Zwillingsvater* (Twins Father) and were given white bread and milk and assured that they wouldn't have to work like the other children, they dried their eyes and wondered if it wouldn't be so bad after all.

UNCLE MENGELE

Later that day, or maybe it was the next, they had a visitor. A handsome, dark-haired man whom they had seen at the ramp, flicking a riding crop to the left and right to indicate which line the new arrivals were destined for. He called out *'Zwillinge heraus!'* (Twins out!) and *'Zwillinge heraustreten!'* (Twins step forward!) and the twins went to him like obedient pupils on their first day at a new school. Some mothers hid their twins beneath their clothes and smuggled them through the other line. They were never seen again.

The dark-haired man hadn't been smiling at the 'selection'. He was too intent on finding twins. But he was smiling now and handing out candy and chocolates to the children he had picked out of the line. He was

dressed immaculately and he talked softly like a favourite uncle. They would call him Uncle Pepi or Uncle Mengele. Maybe it wouldn't be so bad here after all.

Of all the Nazi war criminals, Dr Josef Mengele must rank as the most depraved and cruel. His barbaric experiments on children, including newborn babies, served no scientific purpose and were indefensible under any circumstances, but what made his crimes so shocking was the fact that he carried out his sadistic experiments not in secret but in full view of his superiors and with their tacit consent.

Auschwitz survivor Alex Dekel recognized a sadist when he saw one.

'I have never accepted the fact that Mengele himself believed he was doing serious work – not from the slipshod way he went about it. He was only exercising his power. Mengele ran a butcher shop – major surgeries were performed without anaesthesia. Once, I witnessed a stomach operation – Mengele was removing pieces from the stomach, but without any anaesthetic. Another time, it was a heart that was removed, again without anaesthesia. It was horrifying. Mengele was a doctor who became mad because of the power he was given.'

The gateway to Auschwitz: Jewish workers turned round the letter Ḃ as a small act of subversion – the Germans never noticed

EARLY SIGNS OF EVIL

His upbringing must have contributed to his depravity. but it wasn't too obvious at first. His family were prosperous and devoutly religious. His father owned a manufacturing business in Bavaria, but was a reserved, unfeeling man and his wife was an ill-tempered harpy who terrorized her husband and his employees. But her three sons, of whom Josef was the eldest, were cheerful, bright and well behaved. However, Josef soon exhibited a degree of fastidiousness in his appearance that indicated an obsessive hygiene fetish. He took to wearing white cotton gloves and became passionate about the spurious science of eugenics, the study of inherited disease and deformity. It has been argued that Mengele's extravagant fastidiousness was consistent with withdrawal and that the lack of empathy he exhibited is frequently seen as 'evil'.

Mengele was not the typical sadist who began by pulling the wings off insects and torturing small animals. His psychosis was an extreme intellectual conceit in which he saw himself as being superior to other people and therefore above moral laws and normal codes of conduct. He was obsessed with his own omnipotence, or the illusion of such power, and he deliberately sought out a situation in which he could exercise the power of life and death.

EDUCATION OF A MONSTER

During his first term at Munich University in 1930 he fell under the spell of Social Darwinist Dr Ernst Rüdin, who indoctrinated Mengele and his fellow students with the idea that mentally disabled and physically deformed people were unworthy of life. It was a doctor's duty, he said, to end that life to save the state the expense, and their families the burden, of caring for them. Rüdin's extreme views brought him to the attention of Hitler who in 1934 invited him to draw up the Protection of Hereditary Health Act, which called for the forced sterilization of persons who exhibited a range of imperfections including simple-mindedness, epilepsy, manic depression and even alcoholism.

Rüdin's absurd theories appealed to Mengele, who saw them as scientific confirmation of his own superiority and as a licence to experiment on 'inferior' human beings, should he ever get the chance to do his own 'research'. When Social Darwinism and eugenics were adopted by the National Socialists to support their belief in the Aryan Master Race, Mengele became a fanatical convert to the new cult. But it was only after

he completed his PhD and was appointed research assistant at the University of Frankfurt that Mengele found the mentor who would encourage him to pursue his obsession with racial purity.

Professor Verschuer impressed on his pupils the necessity for studying twins who, he believed, held the secret of heredity. If twins shared the same genetic make-up, he argued, it should be possible to conduct experiments which demonstrated that heredity rather than environment determined an individual's psychological and physical development. Verschuer petitioned for Mengele to be awarded a grant to fund his research and encouraged him to request a posting to Auschwitz. On his arrival Mengele was appointed physician to the sub-camp of Birkenau, but soon gave the impression that he was a senior physician by his energy and enthusiasm.

MORBID OBSESSIONS

According to Professor Robert Lifton, distinguished professor of psychiatry and psychology at the City University of New York, it was as if Mengele had found his calling. In addition to his obsession with twins, Mengele had a morbid fascination with a condition known as heterochromia, which creates eyes of different colours. When he found individuals with this condition he removed the eyes and sent them to

Richard Baer, Josef Mengele and Rudolf Hoess take time out from their labours at Auschwitz concentration camp

Professor Verschuer to study and preserve in his new post at the Berlin-Dahlem Institute of Racial Biology. Mengele saw no ethical reason why he should not try to replicate the effect in living subjects by injecting methylene blue into the eyes of child prisoners.

Ironically, by indulging in these inhumane experiments and performing unnecessary surgery and spinal injections on healthy human beings without anaesthetic, Mengele revealed himself to be the deviant. What was he thinking when he took Gypsy twins for a ride in his car and gave them sweets only to stop at the gas chamber and force them inside?

TWO DISTINCT SELVES

Professor Lifton believes he has identified the process by which intelligent individuals like Mengele justify their aberrant behaviour. He calls it 'doubling' and it involves the individual unconsciously creating 'a new self' to adapt to their 'evil environment'. Lifton acknowledges that Mengele possessed 'unusually intense destructive potential', but feels that he exhibited no signs of aberrant behaviour before he was assigned to the camp and given authority to conduct his experiments.

> '*It was the coming together of the man and the place, the "fit" between the two, that created the Auschwitz Mengele.*'

These inner divisions were reflected in what one inmate described as his 'dead eyes'. Several former prisoners recalled that Mengele avoided eye contact. One inmate doctor referred to Mengele as 'the double man' who appeared to possess 'all the human feelings, pity and so on', but also an 'impenetrable, indestructible cell, which is obedience to the received order'. It is Professor Lipton's contention that Mengele's apparent affection for the children was genuine and part of his former self, but that when it came time to carry out his official function he had no hesitation in killing and dissecting the still warm bodies of the infants he had only moments before patted on the head and even played with. Mengele's behaviour resembled an extreme form of the public and private face of a politician or celebrity. Had he lived to face the enormity of his crimes, he would no doubt have seen nothing odd in having acted in this way.

DR JOSEF MENGELE

BORN: 16 March, 1911, Günzburg, Bavaria
DIED: 7 February, 1979, Bertioga, São Paolo, Brazil
NICKNAME: The Angel of Death, The White Angel, Uncle Pepi

Family: Father: Karl Mengele, factory owner; mother: Walburga (née Hupfauer); siblings: Karl and Alois (Josef was the eldest); wives: Irene (divorced 1954, stayed in Germany with son Rolf), Martha (widow of deceased brother); children: Rolf (by Irene), Karl-Heinz (son of Martha)

Career/life: Potentially successful academic, but joined Nazi Party in 1937, and SS in 1938, when medical degree obtained; decorated hero in Waffen-SS medical service, 1940–42; posted to Race and Resettlement Office, then Birkenau, 1943, where experiments were performed on inmates, often children; transfer to Gross Rosen camp, 1945; escaped to South America; his possible remains exhumed in 1995

Description: Handsome, well-dressed, calm, always smiling; 'Uncle Mengele' to the twins he experimented on – he played with them and seemed to like them, but calmly left many of them dead or deformed

'*He professed to do what he did in the name of science, but it was a madness on his part.*'
Alex Dekel

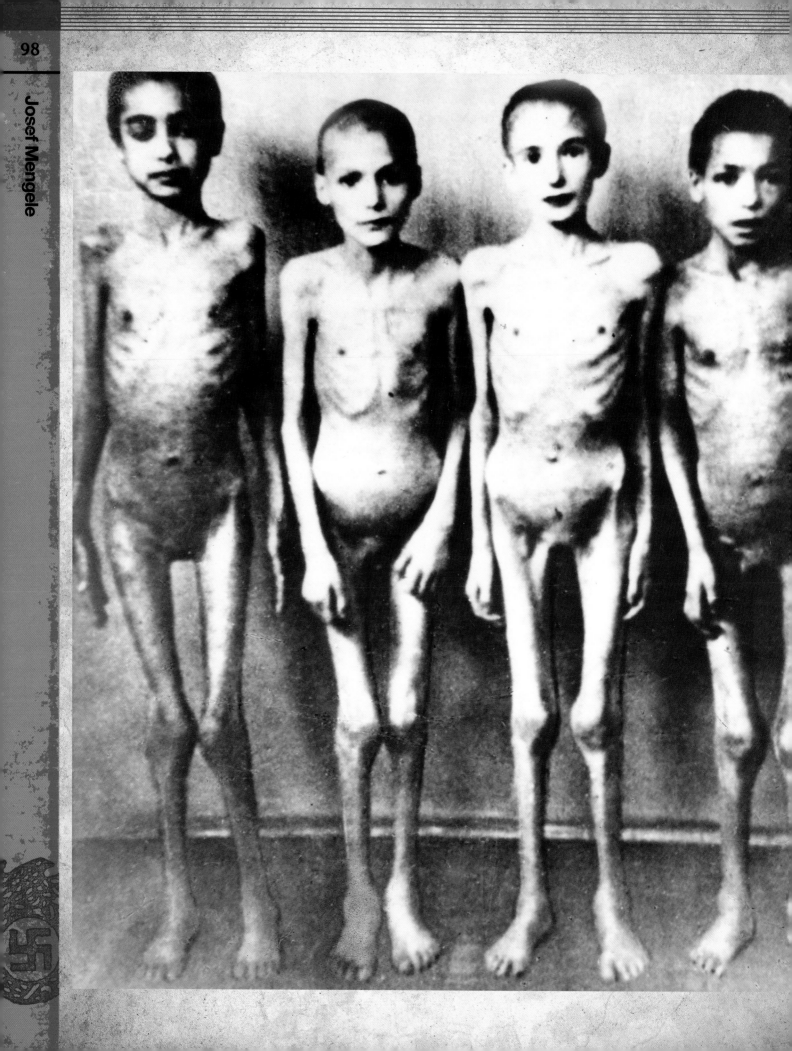

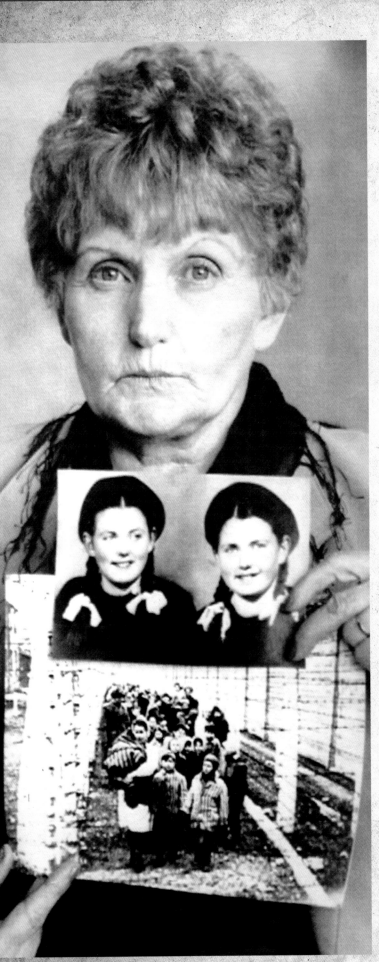

It was mannered and narcissistic like the flamboyant display of a celebrity flaunting their omnipotence before the mass of lesser mortals. It was most evident when Mengele appeared for the daily selection process.

He stood smiling and whistling a cheerful melody in his white physician's coat, his arms outstretched to separate those who would live and those who were to be dispatched to the gas chambers. His appearance earned him the name 'The Angel of Death', but to the youngest of the twins he played the protective parent, isolating them from the horrors of the main camp, although they could hear the screams and smell the fumes from the crematoria.

Professor Lifton concluded,

'The psychological traits Mengele brought to Auschwitz exist in many of us, but in him they took exaggerated form. His impulse toward omnipotence and total control of the world around him were means of fending off anxiety and doubt, fears of falling apart – ultimately, fear of death. That fear also activated his sadism and extreme psychic numbing. He could quiet his fears of death in that death-dominated environment by performing the ultimate act of power over another person: murder.'

FAR LEFT: Romany twins who were victims of Mengele's experiments, supposedly conducted to discover the secret of multiple births

LEFT: Eva Mozer Kor with a picture of her twin sister. Both survived Auschwitz and here she is protesting at proposals to study data gained through Nazi experiments

Leni Riefenstahl

A Wonderful, Terrible Life

'Reality doesn't interest me.'

Leni Riefenstahl (born Hélène Bertha Amalie), the high-spirited daughter of a wealthy Berlin businessman, was always determined to do what she wanted and damn the consequences. When her parents forbade her to enrol in dance classes at the age of 16, she did so anyway and only agreed to leave when her father threatened divorce.

Barely out of her teens, she toured Europe as a 'free' dancer under the auspices of Max Reinhardt and seemed destined for a glittering career until a knee injury forced her to abandon the stage at the age of 22. Undeterred by this setback, she then found fame as a glamorous movie actress after tracking down Arnold Fanck, the director of her favourite film, *Mountain of Destiny*, and persuading him that she could be his muse. She may have had an ulterior motive for flattering Fanck, for it wasn't only his film that she was enamoured with; it was the male star Luis Trenker. She would have a passionate affair with him. But she was genuinely fascinated by the art of film-making and persuaded Fanck to teach her how to use filters and experimental film stock to invest the natural landscape with an epic grandeur.

> 'I started to become excited about working with the camera. I was interested in lenses, in celluloid, in the filter technique... the editing room became a magic workshop for me.'

DIRECTORIAL DEBUT

Fanck's melodramatic adventure films celebrated the mystical attraction of formidable mountains and the heroes who risked their lives to conquer them. So Riefenstahl mastered mountaineering and skiing to convince the director that she was able to cope with the physical demands of the roles. Their collaborations, which included *The White Hell of Pitz Palu* (1929), caught the public imagination at the height of the Depression, when German audiences demanded escapism, and their popularity made her a star of German silent cinema, leading one critic to dub her 'Hitler's pin-up girl'.

However, once she had learned all Fanck could teach her and had sensed that his career was threatened by his refusal to make propaganda films for the new Nazi regime, she seized her chance to star in and direct her own series of 'mountain' films. Her first feature, *The Blue Light* (1932), was awarded the Silver Medal at the Venice Film festival that year and brought her international recognition.

MESMERIZED BY HITLER

She was indomitable, courageous and the personification of Nordic beauty. It was said that she had climbed crags in her bare feet and had survived a near-fatal avalanche, which only made her more determined to reach the summit. But it was her gushing fan letter to the Führer that elicited an invitation to tea with him, shortly after his accession to the chancellorship in 1933.

She had, by her own admission, been 'mesmerized' by a speech Hitler had given in Berlin earlier that year and had been sold on the myth of Aryan supremacy after reading *Mein Kampf*.

> 'The book made a tremendous impression on me. I became a confirmed National Socialist after reading the first page. I felt a man who could write such a book would undoubtedly lead Germany. I felt very happy that such a man had come.'

In later years, Riefenstahl claimed that she had no special regard for Hitler, but photographs taken on the day of their first meeting capture a young woman clearly in adoration of the man who was dominating events in Europe by his personality and would soon do so by force.

In 1937 she told the *Detroit News*, 'Hitler is the greatest man who ever lived. He truly is without fault, so simple and at the same time possessed of masculine strength.'

FILM-MAKER TO THE REICH

After the war, when her association with the regime had made her a pariah in the film industry, she would state that she had only agreed to make a Nazi rally film, *Triumph of the Will* (1935), on the understanding that Hitler would not ask her to film another (as if Hitler would be dictated to by anyone, especially a woman). However, *Triumph of the Will*, which documented the 1934 Nuremberg rally, was not the only film about a Nazi rally that she had made. Just months after her first meeting with Hitler she had produced *Victory of Faith* (1933), an undistinguished effort that failed to be given the dictator's approval and was confined to the vaults for forty years.

When she was commissioned to make *Triumph of the Will*, therefore, she planned and orchestrated her shots meticulously months in advance so as not to risk disappointing the Führer again. She did not. Visually impressive and masterfully executed, her film remains highly regarded among cineastes, film critics and film school students for its technical achievements, though repulsive in its glorification of the fascist aesthetic. At its premiere Hitler presented its director with a bouquet of lilac and declared her to be the 'perfect German woman'.

LENI RIEFENSTAHL

BORN: 22 August, 1902, Berlin, Germany
DIED: 8 September, 2003, Pöcking, Bavaria
NICKNAME: Hitler's Film-maker

Family: Born to prosperous Protestant family, businessman father; husband: Peter Jacob (1944–46) – she is also rumoured to have married her partner, Horst Kettner, 40 years her junior, in 2003, when she was 101 years old

Career/life: Starred in a number of films for Arnold Fanck; directed first film in 1932; first met Hitler in 1933; filmed Nazi Party rallies, 1933–35, Olympic Games, 1936, at Hitler's behest; present at invasion of Poland, filmed Nazi victory parade; used concentration camp inmates in film, 1940–42, who were subsequently sent to Auschwitz; left Berlin in 1945 and spent three years in various detention centres; her 1950s film-making attempts met with resistance; 1960s photographs of Nuba tribe in Africa became best-selling books in the 1970s; photographed celebrities such as Mick Jagger in 1970s; achieved underwater photography success, 1978–2002

Description: Beautiful and multi-talented, began as a dancer and actress, then became Germany's best-known film-maker and a successful photographer; surrounded by opposition and protest because she was a fervent Nazi sympathizer; noted for enormous stamina and longevity; made her last film at the age of 100

'I am one of the millions who thought Hitler had all the answers.'

LENI RIEFENSTAHL DOSSIER

› Riefenstahl coveted the leading role in Sternberg's *The Blue Angel* (1930), but lost out to her rival, Marlene Dietrich.

› She spent the war years as a frontline correspondent and witnessed the massacre of Polish civilians in Koskie, but despite her revulsion she filmed Hitler's entry into Warsaw just weeks later.

› Her film of the opera *Tiefland* never saw completion. It was alleged that she used Gypsies from a concentration camp as extras and promised them their freedom in return, allegations she strenuously denied. Survivors later identified them and said they had all been gassed at Auschwitz, although Riefenstahl maintained she met them after the war.

› After the war Riefenstahl reinvented herself as a stills photographer, taking shots of celebrities such as Mick Jagger and his new wife Bianca for glossy magazines.

› In the 1960s she lived for six months with a primitive tribe in southern Sudan so that she could document their body painting culture and rituals.

› At the age of 71 she took up scuba diving to become an underwater photographer, lying about her age to qualify for the certificate.

Following complaints of under-representation from the German military, she returned to Nuremberg in 1935 and directed the short film *Day of Freedom* (1935), which included many shots of the German forces. It was at the 1935 Nuremberg rally that the insidious Nuremberg Laws were introduced, laws which legitimized the regime's racist ideology and paved the way for the mass murder of millions of enemies of the Reich.

It was Riefenstahl's defence that she had no choice but to put her talents to the service of the regime, but other film-makers such as Fritz Lang and Billy Wilder had emigrated to Europe and America rather than provide propaganda for a dictatorship. Her claim to have remained in Germany in order to fight anti-Semitism rang hollow when it was learned that not only had she never raised a finger to do so, or spoken out against the regime, but she had denounced her Jewish co-writer, Béla Balázs, to the notorious Jew-baiter Julius Streicher. She had then removed both Balázs's name and that of her Jewish producer, Harry Sokal, from the credits of the 1938 reissue of *The Blue Light*.

Two years later she sold her talents to the regime again, documenting the 1936 Berlin Olympics with funding from Goebbels' Propaganda Ministry.

SHUNNED BY HOLLYWOOD

The resulting documentary *Olympia* (1936), which took her two years to edit, established the template for future sports films with its innovative use of multiple camera set-ups, slow motion, cranes for overhead shots and rails to obtain fluid tracking shots. It was premiered for Hitler's 49th birthday and was rapturously received at international film festivals, but if she expected her consummate artistry to be sufficient to win her invitations to the Hollywood studios, she was rudely mistaken. During a promotional visit to New York in November 1938 she was incensed to learn that all but two Hollywood film-makers refused to receive her, the exceptions being silent comedy producer Hal Roach and Walt Disney. When informed that none of the Jewish studio moguls would allow her on the lot because of the events of Kristallnacht earlier that week (when 30,000 Jews were sent to concentration camps and more than 1,000 synagogues were burned to the ground), she vowed to remain in the US until 'this damn Jewish thing is no longer in the headlines'.

Leni Riefenstahl on location filming *Triumph of the Will in* Nuremberg in 1934: Hitler stands stiffly behind her

UNAPOLOGETIC

Riefenstahl, self-absorbed and contemptuous of her critics, would be smeared with the stigma of Nazism until her death at the age of 101, for no amount of vehement denials would absolve her of guilt by association.

She remained stubbornly unapologetic to the end declaring, 'Work and peace are the only messages of *Triumph of the Will*.'

But even if an artist is not accountable for the use to which their art is put, they are surely accountable to their conscience for what they say in public.

In June 1940 Riefenstahl sent a telegram to Hitler congratulating him on the fall of France, which reveals her true feelings long after she had ceased to curry favour as 'Hitler's favourite film-maker'.

> *'With indescribable joy, deeply moved and filled with burning gratitude, we share with you, my Führer, your and Germany's greatest victory, the entry of German troops into Paris. You exceed anything human imagination has the power to conceive, achieving deeds without parallel in the history of mankind. How can we ever thank you?'*

The VIP rostrum on the opening day of the Berlin Olympics, 1936: Leni Riefenstahl can be seen recording proceedings (top right)

Ernst Roehm

Too Powerful to Live

'Since I am an immature and wicked man, war and unrest appeal to me more than the good bourgeois order. Brutality is respected. The people need wholesome fear. They want to fear something. They want someone to frighten them and make them shudderingly submissive... They need something that will give them a thrill of horror.'

Ernst Roehm was destined to die a violent death and on 2 July 1934 he was murdered in Stadelheim Prison on the orders of his former friend and comrade-in-arms Adolf Hitler, having refused to commit suicide.

'If Adolf wants me dead,' he told his executioners, 'let him do his own dirty work.' It was Nazi justice, sudden, predetermined and pitiless.

Roehm had marched home from the trenches in 1918 at the head of a column of bellicose and brutish thugs, who were returning from a war they had not finished fighting and which they were determined to continue in the beer halls and streets of Bavaria, then a breeding ground for extreme nationalism. Captain Roehm, the third son of a railway worker, was not a revolutionary at that time. He had no ideals to fight for. He organized the SA (*Sturmabteilung*) or Storm Troopers, a paramilitary organization under the banner of patriotism, but their purpose was to mete out brutal retribution for what he and his men saw as the betrayal of the undefeated German Army.

BURNING AMBITION

Roehm was sickened by the shame of having lost a war he was certain could have been won and was disgusted at the cowardice shown by his spineless superiors. Fearing a Bolshevik revolution like the one that had toppled the Czar of Russia the year before, robbing the aristocracy of their lands and titles, the High Command had persuaded the Kaiser to accept the humiliating terms of surrender and the dishonour of abdication.

And Roehm bitterly resented them for it.

Twice he had been severely wounded and had been awarded an Iron Cross First Class for his courage. He would rather have fallen in battle than skulk home in defeat, but he couldn't fight on alone. He would return to Germany and raise an army of his own if need be, to win back his honour and recover the territories stolen under the terms of the hated Versailles Treaty. His Brownshirt militia would tear down the rotten edifice of the Weimar Republic and crush the communists who were waging civil war in the streets and making fools of the new government, who seemed powerless to control them. It was a burning ambition he shared with his former comrade, Corporal Hitler, whom he called Adolf and addressed with the informal 'du', the only Nazi to be permitted that privilege.

EMBARRASSMENT TO THE CAUSE

Both men were embittered and enraged to think that German blood had been shed in vain, but after the ignominious failure of the Munich Putsch in November 1923 the former Bavarian Army corporal was shrewd enough to realize that real and lasting power could not be seized by force alone. The hearts and minds of the people had to be won over and those who couldn't be persuaded would have to be bought with empty promises. As a last resort some would need to be strong-armed into seeing sense – and that

Ernst Roehm was the leader of the SA, which specialized in beer hall brawls – a key tactic in the early days of the Nazis

is where Roehm, co-founder and commander of the 500,000-strong SA, was to prove useful.

Roehm was squat, coarse and uncomplicated. He didn't think too hard or too much about politics. And he didn't give a damn who he offended. He ridiculed the pseudo-mystical Aryan 'philosophy' of Alfred

ERNST ROEHM

BORN: 28 November, 1887, Munich, Bavaria
DIED: 2 July, 1934, Stadelheim Prison, Munich
NICKNAME: The Machine Gun King of Bavaria

Family: Father: Julius Roehm, a railway official, was a strict disciplinarian; mother: Emilie; he was the youngest of three children

Career/life: Joined the Bavarian Army in 1906 and was commissioned in 1908; fought with distinction in the First World War; served in the Reichswehr 1918–23; joined the DAP/NSDAP, 1919, then became Hitler's ally; arrested after the Munich Putsch, 1924; began to rebuild the SA, then resigned in 1925 and took post in Bolivia, 1928–30; recalled by Hitler to head the SA, which he greatly expanded; made cabinet minister, 1933; demanded SA–Reichswehr merger, 1934; the growing strength of the SA, coupled with Roehm's other activities, led to Hitler ordering his death

Description: Portly and battle-scarred street-fighter, undisguised homosexual; became an uncompromising revolutionary whose SA threatened the German army and Hitler himself, but his tactics and lifestyle were universally opposed

'Hitler can't walk over me as he might have done a year ago; I've seen to that. Don't forget that I have three million men, with every key position in the hands of my own people'

Rosenberg in public to the discomfort of true believers such as Himmler and he flaunted his preference for the company of hard-drinking, handsome athletic men to the embarrassment of the army High Command. They demanded that Hitler deal with him before the Reichswehr (forerunner of the Wehrmacht) took an oath of allegiance to their new Commander-in-chief.

Roehm had desired a military career from childhood and didn't see why his sexuality should interfere with his progress through the ranks. He had no respect for anyone who had not been in uniform and openly despised German civilians, whom he condemned as 'swine'.

But he wasn't too discreet and rumours of his 'unnatural' inclinations and those of his men were becoming a concern to the General Staff. Breaking a few heads was to be tolerated in such turbulent times, but blatant displays of homosexuality were taboo and threatened to tarnish the image of the army, even though the SA were not officially part of the regular armed forces.

GROWING SA THREAT

By 1932 the SA had become a terrorist organization, bombing buildings and sowing anarchy throughout the state. Within a year it had grown so large that the army High Command considered the paramilitary divisions to be a serious threat to law and order.

Hitler's reassurances that the SA were merely the political education arm of the Party were disregarded as Roehm called for the amalgamation of the SA and the Reichswehr. The combined force would then be strong enough to stage a new revolution to crush the communists and wrest power from the Weimar government.

He became increasingly frustrated after Hitler began courting the aristocracy, industrialists, financiers and landowners whose support would be crucial to the Party's increasing fortunes. Roehm argued that the Party should be true to its socialist origins and back, by force if necessary, workers' strikes against unscrupulous bosses. He was severely critical of his former friend, whom he now called an artist, a dreamer and, worst of all, a civilian.

RIGHT: Adolf Hitler takes the salute at Franzen Field, Brunswick. Behind him is Roehm

OVERLEAF: Convicted after the 1923 Munich Putsch: (l to r) Pernet, Weber, Frick, Kriebel, Ludendorff, Hitler, Bruckner, Roehm, Wagner

HITLER HAD TO ACT

In February 1934 Hitler attempted to placate Roehm by offering the SA the responsibility for border policing and the premilitary training of youth, but Roehm refused outright. 'What that ridiculous corporal says means nothing to us,' he said. 'I have not the slightest intention of keeping this agreement. Hitler is a traitor, and at the very least must go on leave... If we can't get there with him, we'll get there without him... Adolf is a swine. He will give us all away. He only associates with reactionaries now. His old friends aren't good enough for him. Getting friendly with the East Prussian generals. They're his cronies now.'

Clearly Hitler would have to act.

Roehm may have been a man without imagination, but he saw what was coming and on the eve of his execution he told his jailers, 'All revolutions devour their own children.'

At the end of the war Goebbels ruefully remarked that the murder of Roehm had been a serious mistake.

> '*What Roehm wanted was, of course, right in itself but in practice it could not be carried through by a homosexual and an anarchist. Had Roehm been an upright solid personality, in all probability some hundred generals rather than some hundred SA leaders would have been shot on June 30.*'

LEFT: Even after execution (during the Night of the Long Knives), the corpse of Ernst Roehm still seems to be attempting a Nazi salute

ERNST ROEHM DOSSIER

› Roehm's homosexual activities and those of his men were an open secret, but it has been alleged that the Nazi movement originated from the homosexual underground in Munich and that the Bratwurst Glöckl beer keller where the early Party meetings were held was a notorious gay meeting place.

› Roehm's use of the familiar 'du' when addressing Hitler was not permitted by even the closest of Hitler's inner circle, suggesting an intimacy between the two men that, some say, may have been sexual in nature.

› In 1919 Roehm ordered Hitler to spy on the fledgling German Workers' Party to see if it was worthwhile funding as a front for the political wing of the army.

› Roehm was one of the earliest members of the German Workers' Party (DAP) and his support was crucial in helping Hitler become president of the Party in 1921.

› In 1928 Roehm served as military adviser in Bolivia, but was summoned back to Munich when Hitler sent him a telegram saying, 'I need you'. Shortly after Roehm's return, membership of the SA increased to over one million.

› Roehm's private letters were published in a Munich newspaper in 1931, in which he detailed his homosexual affairs. It was a great embarrassment to

Hitler, whose party was being publicly accused by its political enemies of harbouring homosexuals, drug addicts and sexual deviants. 'The disgusting hypocrisy that the Party demonstrates,' said the editorial, 'outward moral indignation while inside its own ranks the most shameless practices prevail... every knowledgeable person knows that inside the Hitler party the most flagrant whorishness contemplated by paragraph 175 (defining homosexuality as a criminal offence) is widespread.'

› Himmler complained to Roehm that SA commanders were chosen because of their sexual orientation and not for their abilities and cited the case of 35-year-old Obergruppenführer Karl Ernst, who had been a hotel doorman and was then given command of a quarter of a million men. 'Does it not constitute a danger to the Nazi movement if it can be said that Nazi leaders are chosen for sexual reasons?'

› Hitler was finally persuaded to act decisively against Roehm after Himmler and Heydrich had fabricated evidence implicating the SA leader in a planned coup funded by 'the old enemy', France.

Hjalmar Schacht

Banking on Hitler

'No one can find his future with us who is not behind Adolf Hitler heart and soul.'

Hjalmar Schacht, Hitler's haughty Minister of Economics and former head of the Reichsbank, received a copy of his indictment on a charge of crimes against peace in his cell at Nuremberg with the demeanour of a schoolmaster whose authority had been questioned. With barely suppressed contempt he made it clear that he expected to be acquitted. 'I am, after all, a banker.' But if he imagined that being a mere financier absolved him of his part in funding Hitler's war he was mistaken.

The honour tribune during the parade for Adolf Hitler's birthday, 20 April 1938, on Unter den Linden, Berlin. Schacht is in his bowler hat

In the opinion of the United States Consul General in Berlin it was Schacht's 'resourcefulness, his complete financial ruthlessness, and his absolute cynicism' that enabled the Nazis to fund their rearmament programme. 'If it had not been for his efforts [...] the Nazi regime would have been unable to maintain itself in power and to establish its control over Germany, much less to create the enormous war machine which was necessary for its objectives in Europe and later throughout the world.'

BRINGING HITLER TO POWER

Schacht, the son of a Danish baroness and a Prussian aristocrat, had a very fluid interpretation of right and wrong when it came to money. During the First World War he had been dismissed from public service for siphoning 500 million francs' worth of Belgian bonds, set aside for reparations, into the Dresdner Bank – which, coincidentally, had been his previous employer. It was this proclivity for unconventional business practices that made him useful to Hitler, who described Schacht as someone with a 'consummate skill at swindling other people'. Once Hitler had assured himself that Schacht wouldn't do the same to him, he invited the arrogant banker to raise funds for his campaign. Though never a card-carrying member of the Party, Schacht was instrumental in bringing Hitler to power by raising considerable sums for the NSDAP from 1926 to 1932. He also played a part in petitioning President Hindenburg to appoint Hitler to the chancellorship in January 1933.

WAR FUNDING

It was said that Schacht objected to the Führer's plans to wage war, but only on the grounds that it would be too expensive. When faced with the dictator's determination to avenge himself on the victorious Allies, who had imposed punitive reparations after the First World War, Schacht devised a plan for funnelling funds into the Reich that could not be disrupted by hostilities.

In 1930 he suggested the establishment of a new clearing house for the world's major banks, which would facilitate payment of Germany's reparations. The Bank for International Settlements (BIS) would be based in Basel, Switzerland and Schacht would be its first president. The appointment was Chancellor Hitler's reward for Schacht's invaluable support during 'the struggle', but once in place Schacht was to use his influence to convince the world's major banks to invest in the regeneration of Germany.

Hitler knew a shady character when he saw one. He didn't trust the banker and was openly offensive towards him. He once said that Schacht couldn't resist 'cheating someone out of 100 marks' if he had the chance, but as the other bankers were 'a bunch of crooks' Schacht was not obliged to be 'scrupulously honest' with any of them.

In the pre-war years Schacht succeeded in channelling vast sums from foreign investors into Germany, with which Hitler funded rearmament and the ambitious programme of public works that earned the grudging admiration of other nations. Even after Hitler's succession to the chancellorship had staunched the flow of capital from Europe and the US, money continued to pour in from pre-existing agreements to the tune of an estimated 294 million Swiss francs.

When Hitler annexed Austria in 1938 and demanded that its gold reserves be transferred to the Reichsbank, the BIS obligingly deposited 22 tons of gold from the Austrian national bank in the regime's account. And as Hitler greedily swallowed up successive countries, he acquired their gold reserves too, even when those accounts were held in trust abroad, because the BIS managed accounts for both the aggressor and the country that had capitulated.

When German troops entered Prague the Bank of England transferred six million pounds in Czech gold reserves to the BIS, which the British could have delayed under the circumstances. But the governor of the Bank of England, Montague Norman, was said to be on very friendly terms with his fellow BIS member Hjalmar Schacht and didn't see any reason to withhold the funds which eventually found their way into the coffers of the Reichsbank.

RELEASED ON APPEAL

After war was declared, Schacht was sidelined for the duration and spent the last year of the conflict in concentration camps, having been accused of participation in the July plot to kill Hitler. Those who had taken part in the attempt denied his involvement. Schacht, they said, was incapable of acting on principles he didn't possess.

After his liberation by the Allies, he was indicted at Nuremberg for having assisted the Nazi military machine, but was acquitted after turning state's evidence against his co-defendants.

He was subsequently convicted of war crimes by a German de-Nazification court and sentenced to eight years in prison. In 1948 he was released on appeal after which he set up his own bank and continued to prosper.

The chief prosecutor, Robert S. Jackson, was clearly offended by Schacht's indifference to the suffering he had facilitated, describing him as,

Men of the Finance Corps, 3rd American Army, examine a hoard of Nazi money hidden in a salt mine in Moeckers, Thüringen

> 'The most dangerous and reprehensible type of all opportunists, someone who would use a Hitler for his own ends, and then claim, after Hitler was defeated, to have been against him all the time. He was part of a movement that he knew was wrong, but was in it just because he saw it was winning.'

HJALMAR SCHACHT

....

BORN: 22 January, 1877, Tinglev, Prussia (now Denmark)

DIED: 3 June, 1970, Munich, Federal Republic of Germany

NICKNAME: The Old Wizard

Family: Father: William Schacht; mother: Baroness Constanze von Eggers; wives: Louise Sowa (1903–40), Manci (1941–70)

Career/life: Joined Dresdner Bank, 1903, became deputy director 1908–15; in charge of First World War purchases in Belgium, dismissed because of irregularities; currency commissioner, Weimar Republic, 1923, when he stabilized the German mark; president of Reichsbank, resigned 1930; NSDAP supporter, 1926 onwards; became Reichsbank president again, 1933; Minister of Economics, 1934; honorary NSDAP member, 1937; resigned as Minister of Economics, 1937, dismissed from Reichsbank, 1939; remained as Minister Without Portfolio until 1943; involved with German Resistance,1938–41, arrested after attempt on Hitler's life, 1944, sent to various camps, liberated by US, 1945; tried and acquitted at Nuremberg, founded own bank in 1953

Description: Wore a pince-nez and high collars, highly conservative, yet daring financial wheeler-dealer; marked by ambition and hubris; turned to fascism early in life and became Nazi apologist, yet confirmed anti-Nazi later on; hostile to Germany's Jews – devised Jewish-financed emigration plans in 1934 and 1938 – but opposed to Nazis' bad treatment of them and spoke out against it at personal risk, or so it has been claimed

'Colonies are necessary to Germany. We shall get them through negotiation if possible; but if not, we shall take them.'

Albert Speer

The Good Nazi?

'Albert Speer was a war criminal. He did commit crimes against humanity and if the prosecutors at the Nuremberg tribunal had known everything about his activities during the Third Reich he would have hung.'

Professor David Cesarani

The 20 years Albert Speer spent in Berlin's Spandau Prison gave him ample time to reflect on the part he had played in Hitler's regime. It was said that his organizational skills had increased armaments production to such a degree that it had given the Nazis the means to extend the war by at least another year, a year in which the conflict claimed hundreds of thousands more lives. But for the former architect, incarceration and isolation had also given him invaluable time to write the memoirs that would make him an international celebrity and a very wealthy man. Just six weeks after his release he was paid 50,000 marks for an exclusive interview with the German weekly news magazine *Der Spiegel*, and that was only the first of many lucrative deals for the man who made a profit from his nefarious past and his association with Adolf Hitler. However, there was one thing Speer secretly yearned for and would be denied to the day he died – the recognition of his talent as an architect and the respect of his fellow professionals.

UNBUILT DESIGNS

Although Speer had mastered the technical aspects of his profession and Hitler had ignominiously failed to be accepted by the Vienna Academy of Fine Arts, the Führer was not resentful, but saw Speer rather as his protégé, a young man who could bring his grandiose vision to life.

'Hitler quite often told me: "You are fulfilling my dream. I would like to have been an architect. Fate made me the bildhauer Deutschlands, the sculptor of Germany. I would have liked to be Germany's architect. But I can't: you are. Even when I am dead you will go on, and I give you all my authority so that even after I am dead you will continue."'

LEFT: Albert Speer listens in on a jovial conversation between Adolf Hitler and his Chief of Staff of the Army, General Kurt Zeitzler
OVERLEAF: Official Third Reich sculptor Arno Breker, appointed to the post by Hitler, works up a larger-than-life bust of his friend Speer, 1942

Ironically, Speer only saw one of his many grand designs built in his lifetime – the palatial new Reich Chancellery in Berlin, beneath which Hitler would commit suicide in his concrete bunker in April 1945. The building stood in what would have been the new capital of the Third Reich, a city of imperial grandeur to be renamed Welthauptstadt Germania. Long broad avenues flanked by massive classical edifices would have converged on the Volkshalle, a domed conference hall three times the height of St Paul's Cathedral. The dome would have contained 180,000 people, all gathered to hear the proclamations of the emperor of the New Order. But Hitler's great modern metropolis would remain a tabletop model and fantasy to be scrutinized by the dictator and his young alter ego even as the bombs and artillery shells shook the plaster from the ceiling of the Chancellery.

PLAYING THE INNOCENT

But if Speer had failed to realize his dreams as an architect, he proved to have a formidable talent for self-promotion and as an actor on the public stage. At Nuremberg after the war he shrewdly accepted some degree of responsibility for his role in the regime, playing the part of the deceived young artist who had fallen under Hitler's spell, feigning remorse so convincingly that the judges spared him the death sentence.

His fellow defendants hated him not only for what they saw as his betrayal of the Führer's memory, but also for being smarter than them in playing the penitent Nazi card before they could think of it. But even if they had adopted his strategy, it's doubtful that any of them could have appeared as convincing, for Speer was a highly educated, well-spoken aristocrat and it is more than likely that his background and bearing played a part in the judges' decision.

EVIDENCE OF GUILT

But unbeknown to the prosecution, in the last days of the war Speer had driven through the night, braving Allied bombs, to recover his treasured art collection from the Brandenburg home of his friend Robert Frank. The next day he deposited the 30 paintings in the vaults of the Commerzbank in Hamburg under his friend's name. It wasn't just their value that he was safeguarding, but the part they could play in undermining his defence in a future trial. The paintings had been bought from a dealer with a dubious reputation for acquiring artworks from Jewish owners

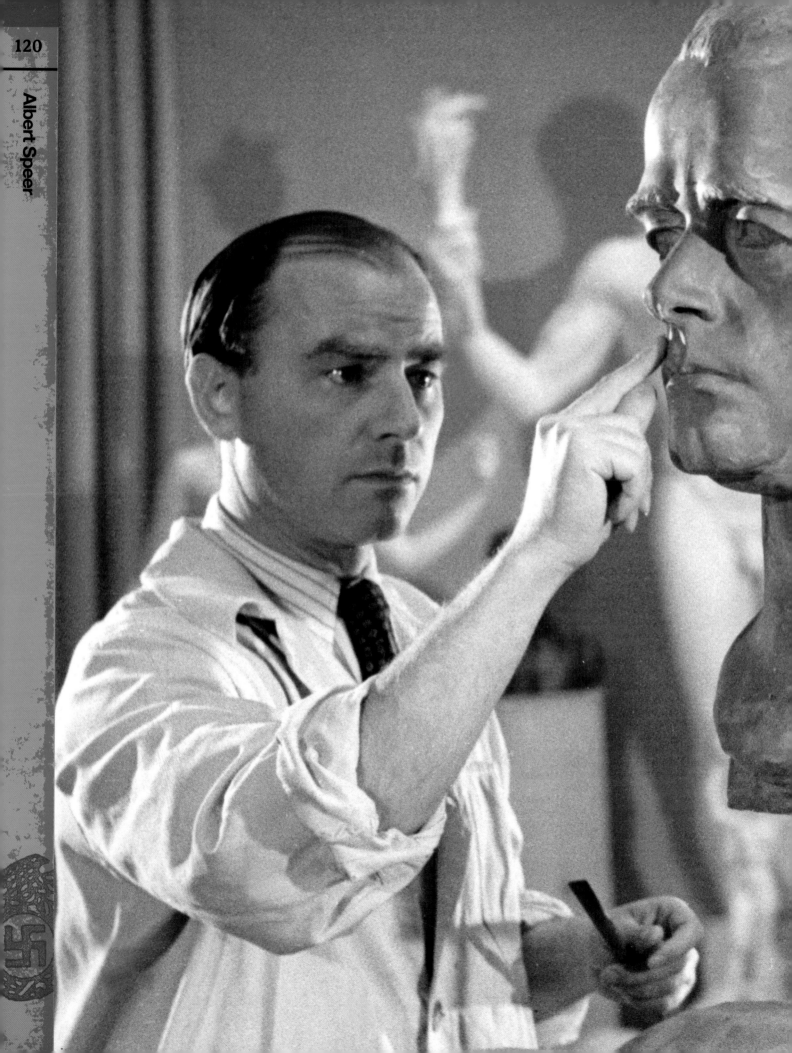

at a fraction of their true value and if Speer could be linked to the stolen paintings he would not be able to play the innocent on the witness stand. He told his interrogators that the paintings had all been lost or destroyed and without them there was little to tie him directly to the crimes.

There was further evidence of Speer's guilt. Speer's former assistant, Rudolf Wolters, had kept detailed records of the 23,765 Jewish apartments that were seized on his orders, causing 75,000 Jews to be 'resettled'. The buildings were to be demolished in preparation for the rebuilding of Berlin. Later Speer wrote to Wolters asking him to delete the passages that implicated him in the operation saying, 'I suggest that the relevant pages no longer exist.' By this time Wolters was so disgusted by Speer's false act of contrition and continual denials that he published the documents to refute the lies.

According to Professor David Cesarani, Speer had used his imprisonment to perfect his alibi. 'He found the perfect formula for taking a degree of responsibility for the atrocities perpetrated by the Third Reich while not accepting personal culpability for them.'

REFORMED NAZI ROLE

On his release from prison in 1965 he perfected the role of the decent, distinguished reformed Nazi who was ready to admit that he had been swept up in the euphoria of the era and now felt foolish and partly responsible for its 'excesses'. He admitted responsibility but assumed no personal guilt. And in so doing he helped exorcize the ghosts of Germany's past. But there were those who were not persuaded that his redemption was genuine and who poured scorn on his claims to have planned to assassinate Hitler in January 1945, plans which he kept entirely to himself until he needed to appear the injured party at Nuremberg. As one sceptic observed, 'Are we to believe the second most powerful figure in the Third Reich was prevented from pouring poison gas into the bunker's ventilation system for the want of a ladder?!'

The Cathedral of Light at Nuremberg 1938, created by Speer using anti-aircraft searchlights at 40-foot (12-m) intervals. 'The effect surpassed anything I had expected,' he said.

ALBERT SPEER

BORN: 19 March, 1905, Mannheim, Baden, Germany
DIED: 1 September, 1981, London, United Kingdom

Family: Upper middle class; father: Albert Speer; mother: Luis; second of three sons; wife: Margarete (née Weber); children: Albert, Hilde, Fritz, Margret, Arnold, Ernst

Career/life: Studied then taught architecture – father and grandfather were architects also; joined Nazi Party in 1931, after attending rallies; given several Nazi renovation commissions and then designed 1933 May Day commemoration; designed 1933 Nuremberg rally; Party's chief architect, 1934, after finding favour with Hitler; General Building Inspector for the Reich Capital, 1937, and government position; produced plans for new Berlin, shelved when war broke out; built new Reich Chancellery in record time, 1938; made Minister of Armaments, 1942, in charge of all wartime production; saves Germany from Hitler's Nero Decree, or scorched-earth policy, 1945; paid final visit to Hitler's bunker, 1945; joined short-lived successor government; arrested by US and tried at Nuremberg, sentenced to 20 years' imprisonment, when he wrote his profitable memoirs

Description: Tall and well-presented, with exceptional architectural and organizational abilities, the debate goes on about his involvement in slave labour and the Holocaust

'I still see my main guilt in my having approved of the persecution of the Jews and of the murder of millions of them.'

ALBERT SPEER DOSSIER

› His biographer, Dan van der Vat, described Speer as 'an emotional cripple' who was bullied by his brothers and treated coldly by his mean, indifferent father and embittered mother. Speer admitted that his ability to manipulate people derived from his 'artificial and uncomfortable' upbringing, which left him reserved and withdrawn.

› While studying at Berlin University in 1925/6 he paid other students to do his drawings as his own draughtsmanship was considered too poor.

› Speer believed that his popularity with the Nazi elite was due to the fact that he was the only person with a private car in the Wannsee district of Berlin at the time and was willing to take Goebbels and other leaders to romantic assignations they didn't want their official drivers to know about.

› Hitler often invited Speer round for dinner. Psychologist Gitta Sereny claimed, 'Both were bedevilled from childhood by thwarted, imagined and withheld love', a deficiency which made them incapable of expressing emotions.

› Speer claimed to have been ignorant of the Holocaust but he attended a meeting in Posen, Poland in 1943 at which Himmler called for the extermination of the Jews. Speer said he left before Himmler gave his speech, but the speech included a direct reference to Speer which incriminated him. 'Of course this has nothing to do with Party member Speer. YOU can't do anything about this.'

› After his release Speer secretly visited a Benedictine monastery, where he confessed his personal involvement in the death of slave workers to Father Athanasius Wolff. He then immediately retracted his confession, suggesting that he could not admit it even to himself.

SHUNNED BY HIS PROFESSION

Speer returned to the Zeppelinfeld at Nuremberg many years after his release, to see the site of his greatest triumph once more. But all he could see were the weeds growing through cracks in the limestone steps leading to the podium where Hitler had given his rabble-rousing speeches. 'The Führer,' he sighed, 'would have been very mad at me for this poor stone quality.'

In the end he betrayed Hitler by selling his mentor's original sketches to finance an affair he is said to have had with a married English woman, the same woman who was allegedly with him the morning he died in a plush London hotel in September 1981, aged 76.

LEFT: View of Hitler's study in the new Reich's Chancellery, Berlin, designed by Speer to give the occupant a sense of self-importance
ABOVE: Albert Speer, Minister in Charge of War Production, inspects the Atlantic Wall which was threatened with imminent attack

Three years before his death Speer consented to be interviewed by the BBC for a programme on the subject closest to his heart, at the end of which he asked the interviewer if he wouldn't mind taking a gift to American architect Philip Johnson, who had designed the AT&T building in New York and whom he greatly admired. When the interviewer presented Johnson with the autographed copy of Speer's portfolio, a look of revulsion crossed his face. He thrust the book under the bench they were sitting on and refused to take it with him when he left the restaurant where they had been having lunch. Had he known of it, Speer would have felt that rebuff more keenly than the clanging of the cell door in Spandau.

but also to make it easier on his own men, who then only had to herd the incoming 'shipment' through the selection process and on to the gas chambers.

SIMPLY OBEYING ORDERS

With his soft mellifluous voice and courteous manners, Franz Stangl challenged the stereotypical image of the strident, arrogant SS officer. Stripped of his white hunting outfit and riding crop and dressed casually in grey flannel trousers, grey sweater, white shirt and tie he presented a deceptively amiable figure to those who visited him in prison after the war. The only intimidating aspect was his physical stature – an imposing six feet (1.83 m). But it was clear, even in the sterile waiting room in Düsseldorf remand prison, that Stangl had been and remained a dominant personality. However, four years in solitary confinement had taken the edge off his arrogance. He admitted to suffering bouts of depression, though he rallied at the thought of attending a literature class and joining the chess club to take his mind off the numbing routine of prison life.

He appeared unconcerned about the outcome of his impending appeal, but it may simply have been relief that, at the age of 63, the running was finally over and he would now have the opportunity to justify his actions and 'clear his name'. When the court heard that he had simply been obeying orders they would surely let him go. Only by living such an illusion could he avoid facing the facts and his part in the killings. He maintained the illusion of normality with a daily routine of exercise

Stangl ended up in a cell of his own, but at least the conditions, though spartan, were humane, unlike those he had enforced

and reading to 'improve his mind'. It was the last in a long line of lies, deceit and deception that he had unconsciously constructed to insulate himself against meeting the monster in the mirror.

NOTHING WRONG WITH MURDER

It began the day he had his name added to a list of Nazi sympathizers to avoid being shot by the Germans when they marched into Austria in 1938. His fellow Linz police officers were being rounded up by the Germans for imprisoning Austrian Nazis, after the Party had been declared illegal in the run-up to annexation. Franz had saved his neck by posing as an illegal Nazi, but his wife Theresa felt it was a betrayal

Russian medics examine an emaciated inmate of a Nazi camp.
Stangl magnified the cruelty against Jews by his devotion to duty

of all that they believed in and wished he had taken his chances instead. He was later to admit that he should have killed himself in 1938 but he didn't have the courage to leave his wife and children, nor did he see why they should be punished for something that was none of their doing.

Having aligned himself with the enemy, he saw nothing wrong in agreeing to the Nazis' next demand by ending his affiliation to the Church, a requirement made of every Austrian official who wished to continue in their profession. For his wife, a regular churchgoer, this was an act of betrayal for which she could never forgive her husband or the Party.

'They do it so subtly you see,' Stangl explained to his interrogator. 'They persuade you to give up all you hold dear one piece at a time – never too much at once – so that it is only later that you realize how far down you have allowed yourself to slide.'

But while he felt that hiding the truth from his family was permissible under the circumstances, he had a harder time convincing himself that participation in mass murder was justifiable. The turning point appears to have come shortly after he was assigned to the Nazi euthanasia department known as T4 at Schloss Hartheim, in November 1940.

He visited an institution for severely handicapped children where he claimed that the Mother Superior pointed out a 16-year-old boy curled up in a basket on the floor and said, 'Just look at him. No good to himself or anyone else. How could they refuse to deliver him from this miserable life?' A priest who was in attendance nodded approval. Stangl claimed that this shook him. 'Here was a Catholic nun, a Mother Superior, and a priest. And they thought it was right. Who was I then to doubt what was being done?'

Their endorsement of Nazi 'mercy killing' let Stangl off the hook as he saw it, for as a Catholic they were his conscience and if they sanctioned such practices, then he reasoned that they must be morally justified.

CLINICAL DETACHMENT

When interviewed by journalist Gitta Sereny he recalled such significant events in his career with clinical detachment as if reviewing the record of an employee. Only rarely did he betray any emotion and it was invariably in connection with having deceived his wife and the realization that each lie he had told her had lost more of her trust and brought him deeper into debt with the regime.

Once he had told one lie it was easier to tell another and another. In the end he couldn't tell a genuine memory from one he had repeated so often that even he believed it. When Theresa asked about his promotion to Sobibor in 1942, he assured her that he was only involved in the construction of the buildings and that it was a forced labour camp. She only found out the truth when one of his colleagues made a drunken confession. Stangl then assured her that the deaths in the camp could be counted in dozens and were unavoidable due to disease and the bad conditions caused by Allied bombing!

IGNORED REALITY

He detached himself from reality by immersing himself in a series of additions to the site.

> 'I repressed it all by trying to create a special place: gardens, new barracks, new kitchens, new everything; barbers, tailors, shoemakers, carpenters. There were hundreds of ways to take one's mind off it; I used them all.'

His principal tactic was denial. He persuaded himself that the prisoners were nothing more than animals.

> 'When I was on a trip once, years later in Brazil, my train stopped next to a slaughterhouse. The cattle in the pens, hearing the noise of the train, trotted up to the fence and stared at the train. They were very close to my window, one crowding the other, looking at me through that fence. I thought then, "Look at this, this reminds me of Poland; that's just how the people looked, trustingly, just before they went into the tins[...]Those big eyes which looked at me not knowing that in no time at all they'd all be dead."'

And all the while he was conscious of the fact that if he didn't carry out his orders he would be sent back to his former posting in the police force where he would have to work under a superior that he detested. It didn't seem to have occurred to him that this disagreeable situation would be infinitely preferable to living with the knowledge that he had facilitated the murder of tens of thousands of innocent people. In his mind he had managed to disconnect his actions from the consequences.

JEWS WERE TO BLAME

The extermination of the Jews and other prisoners was seen as a necessary evil and the first stage in creating a New Order in Europe. It wasn't murder, it was ethnic cleansing, and comparable to a surgeon who cuts out a tumour in order that the patient can live.

He refused to take responsibility. The Jews weren't blameless, he argued. They weren't all innocent. The wealthier ones could have saved the poor ones had they shared their possessions, the trustees could have refused to participate in the processing of new arrivals. God had willed it so the Jews could have their own homeland. It was everyone's fault but his. He didn't hate the Jews, he despised them for submitting to their fate like lemmings.

Aged 62, Franz Stangl is escorted into court in Düsseldorf to face trial on charges of murdering over 900,000 people, 1970

> 'They were so weak; they allowed everything to happen, to be done to them... that is how contempt is born. I could never understand how they could just give in as they did.'

He had never hurt anyone, he protested. The Holocaust wasn't committed out of hatred. It was to rob the Jews of their wealth and influence. It was all about money. And he should know. He stole the possessions of those he had hounded into the gas chambers, which amounted to 145 kilograms of gold and 4,000 carats in diamonds by the time he left Treblinka. The loot was deposited in SS bank accounts.

ONLY DOING HIS DUTY

He excused himself from responsibility by insisting that he had found himself in the wrong place at the wrong time and that anyone would have acted as he had done if they found themselves in the same situation. He spoke with pride of his efficiency, the long hours he had put in, the personal sacrifices he had made. Then he went on about his devotion to his work and his aversion to the coarse language and drunkenness of his colleagues, as if distancing himself from the workers in a factory in which he had been the foreman. The months at Treblinka were 'the happy times', he said, and he had even kept a daily journal detailing the improvements he had introduced – but never his feelings, which he evidently had under firm control.

He kept his cell as neat and orderly as he had his own quarters at the camp. Fastidiously tidy, his fine sensibilities, affected or genuine, were easily offended. But the most offensive thing to him was the assumption of his guilt, that he could be capable of criminality. As a devout Catholic and a former police officer, he could not reconcile the outside world's understanding of him with his own self-image – that of the dutiful servant of the state who had merely carried out his orders to the best of his ability.

He had been coerced into carrying out those terrible things he had been accused of. It was only at the end of the final interview, just hours before his death, that he appeared to have glimpsed the enormity of what he had participated in.

> '*I have never intentionally hurt anyone, myself, but I was there. So yes, in reality I share the guilt... Because my guilt... my guilt, is that I am still here. That is my guilt.*'

Simon Wiesenthal (with moustache), the Austrian-Jewish Nazi-hunter responsible for tracking down Stangl, observes his trial

Rudolf Hess

The Day Hitler's 'Yes-man' Took Flight

'He knew and was capable of understanding Hitler's inner mind, his hatred of Soviet Russia, his lust to destroy Bolshevism, his admiration for Britain and earnest wish to be friends with the British Empire, his contempt for most other countries. No one knew Hitler better or saw him more often in his unguarded moments.'

Winston Churchill, History of the Second World War

When Rudolf Hess, Hitler's former deputy, appeared in the dock at Nuremberg, hesitant, uncertain and confused, he gave the impression that he was suffering from some form of mental disorder. He even denied knowing his fellow defendants. Whether he was feigning or not, it did not save him from receiving a life sentence and he ended his days as the sole inmate of Spandau Prison in a state as close to insanity as one is likely to come across.

During a psychological assessment to gauge if he was fit to stand trial, Hess admitted to simulating memory loss and was diagnosed by the prison psychiatrist Dr Kelley as a 'self-perpetuated hysteric'. But it was Kelley's belief that Hess may well have been suffering from temporary memory loss as his behaviour throughout the trial had been odd, to say the least.

He was a hypochondriac who suffered severe stomach pains whenever he was under stress or sought sympathy from his accusers. But at times he would appear lucid and capable of understanding the charges levelled against him. If he was truly insane it was the same form of insanity – a detachment from reality – that he shared with his fellow defendants, whom he despised.

'It is just incomprehensible how those things came about,' he said when the indictment was handed to him. 'Every genius has the demon in him. You can't blame him [*Hitler*] – it is just in him... It is all very tragic.'

EARLY SIGNS OF INSANITY

Hess may have been unstable from the start. In Nazi newsreels he always appeared agitated, edgy or over-eager to be seen as the Führer's indispensable right-hand man. His public speeches verged on the hysterical as he attempted to whip up the same excitement that only Hitler could generate. And when Hitler spoke Hess could be seen gazing adoringly at his Führer in a way that suggested more than admiration. The German people didn't know what to make of him. With his thick bushy eyebrows, manic stare and fixed smile he made them feel uneasy, but if the Führer trusted him, they reasoned, he must be all right. Unknown to them, Hitler confessed that he valued Hess's servile obedience but found him a wearisome companion.

'Every conversation with Hess,' he complained, 'becomes an unbearably tormenting strain.'

Hess wasn't the brightest button in the box. His own teacher, Professor Haushofer, described him as slow, over-emotional and unimaginative with a tendency to pursue bizarre ideas.

BIZARRE FLIGHT TO SCOTLAND

Hess certainly had his eccentricities – such as his obsession with herbal remedies and horoscopes, which he shared with Himmler – but he would always take it to extremes. On one occasion he asked Nazi leaders to send sacred soil from their region to sprinkle under his baby son's cot. Goebbels couldn't resist offering to send a pavement slab from a street in Berlin.

But when Hess saw that Bormann was usurping his privileged position as Hitler's private secretary, he conceived a plan to win back the Führer's favour. He

Hess sits next to Hermann Goering during the Nuremberg Trials. In the same row are (l to r) Von Ribbentrop, Keitel and Kaltenbrunner

would fly to Scotland to broker a separate peace deal with the British so that Germany would be free to invade Russia without having to fight a war on two fronts.

After parachuting into a farmer's field on 10 May 1941 he demanded to be taken to see the Duke of Hamilton, insisting that he was privy to the peace plan and was expecting him. Naturally, the farmer and the local constabulary assumed he was insane. After his injuries were treated and he had been interrogated by British intelligence he was turned over to psychiatrist Dr Henry Dicks of London's Tavistock Clinic, who must have thought that Christmas had come early that year.

Hess stands next to Viktor Lutze, commander of the SA, as Hitler takes the salute at the 1938 Reich Party Conference

RUDOLF HESS

BORN: 26 April, 1894, Alexandria, Egypt

DIED: 17 August, 1987, Spandau, West Berlin, West Germany

NICKNAME: Fräulein Hess, Fräulein Anna, Black Bertha

Family: Father: Fritz Hess, wealthy merchant with summer home in Germany; mother: Clara (née Münch); siblings: Alfred, Margarete; married Ilse Pröhl in 1927; one son, Wolf

Career/life: Studied in Egypt, Germany and Switzerland, destined to be a merchant; served in Bavarian Army in First World War with distinction; qualified as pilot, flew often later in career; joined Thule Society, 1918, and anti-Semitic Freikorps, then studied at University of Munich; joined NSDAP in 1920, after hearing Hitler speak, and protected him from a bomb, 1921; joined SA, 1922; incarcerated with Hitler after Munich Putsch; deputy leader of NSDAP, 1934, second in succession to Hitler, 1939; flew to Scotland in 1941, on a peace mission, arrested, sentenced to life imprisonment at Nuremberg, mystery 'suicide' in cell

Description: Shy, insecure, seen by some as somewhat effeminate, but distinguished himself as a street-fighter in his early days; a devoted follower rather than a leader; behaviour became increasingly unstable during imprisonment by British, though some Nazis had always thought it so

'My coming to England in this way is, as I realize, so unusual that nobody will easily understand it.'

ACUTE PARANOIA DIAGNOSIS

Dicks found the Deputy Führer sullen but willing to answer questions, presumably hoping that if he was thought to be sincere he would get to meet the duke and make his case for an honourable British surrender. But when it became apparent that his captors had no intention of agreeing to his request, Hess became irritable and unco-operative. He evaded probing questions by claiming to have lost his memory (though he hadn't sustained a head injury after baling out of his plane), picked at his food which he feared might be poisoned and popped homeopathic pills by the handful. Dicks diagnosed acute paranoia.

Hess's discomfort became acute once the psychiatrist raised the question of sexuality. Being a Freudian, Dr Dicks sought the answer to his patients' neuroses in the repression of their sexual desires and he would have been familiar with the rumour that Hess was a transsexual whose cross-dressing habit had earned him the nickname Black Bertha. Whether this was nothing more than idle gossip or black propaganda is not known, but by merely raising the subject Dr Dicks had pressed his patient's buttons.

SUICIDE BIDS

Thereafter Hess attempted suicide twice, once by jumping from a height and the second time by stabbing himself with a bread knife, but he only succeeded in damaging a knee and inflicting a flesh wound on his chest.

During his imprisonment Hess was allowed to write to his wife and in one letter, dated 15 January 1944, he took the opportunity to explain why he had so little to tell her.

'I have been sitting here for literally several hours, wondering what I can write to you about. But I get no further; and that I regret to say is for a very special reason. Since sooner or later, you will notice it or find out about it, I may as well tell you: I have completely lost my memory. The reason for it I do not know. The doctor gave me a lengthy explanation, but I have meanwhile forgotten what it was.'

KARL HAUSHOFER DOSSIER

> Hess's former professor, Karl Haushofer, was a shadowy but significant influence on Hitler's political thinking. At Hess's invitation, his former teacher visited Hitler in Landsberg Prison in 1924 and taught him the principles of geopolitics 'as a weapon to reawaken Germany to fulfil its destined greatness'.

> The professor's contribution to *Mein Kampf* was considerable.

> Haushofer introduced the idea of *Lebensraum* (living space), which became Hitler's excuse for seizing territories which had formerly belonged to Germany and it was Haushofer who shaped racist Nazi rhetoric so it would appeal to the middle and upper classes.

> He convinced the beer keller provocateur that he should make himself more presentable to the middle and upper classes by toning down his rabble-rousing image, discarding his riding crop and swapping his Bavarian lederhosen for more conventional attire.

> Hitler became a vegetarian on the professor's advice and took to drinking sweet tea instead of beer before a long speech, so that he would remain in control of his emotions.

> In 1933, Haushofer's son Albrecht, a government advisor, became a second-class citizen due to his mother's Jewish father. After the intervention of Hess, he was made an 'honorary Aryan'.

> Albrecht was so ashamed of his father's support for Hitler that he conspired to kill the dictator and was executed for his part in the failed July plot.

Moment of glory for Rudolf Hess as he descends the red carpet ahead of assorted dignitaries during a state visit to Rome

Wilhelm Keitel

The Man Who was Hitler's Lackey

'How in heaven's name can they accuse me of conspiring to wage aggressive war when I was nothing but the mouthpiece to carry out the Führer's wishes? As Chief of Staff I had no authority whatsoever – no command function – nothing.'

ield Marshal Keitel, the eldest son of a middle-class landowner, was a battle-hardened professional soldier who considered it his duty to obey his commander-in-chief, be he Kaiser or Führer, but the man behind the medals was not a born soldier and he was scorned by his fellow senior officers as a sycophantic toady to Hitler. He was nicknamed 'Lakeitel' (a pun on the German word for a lackey) and his judgement, both strategic and political, was poor.

POOR JUDGEMENT

Prior to the invasion of Poland Keitel rebutted the advice given by the other commanders, who warned Hitler that the invasion was certain to ignite a world war. The British, said Keitel, were too decadent, the Americans apathetic and the French too degenerate to oppose the Wehrmacht.

Some of the generals considered his assessment of the military situation to be so unrealistic that they ignored his orders at the risk of being reported to Hitler. Others objected to what they saw as his endorsement of the notorious Barbarossa and Night and Fog directives to kill captured commandos, POWS, resistance fighters and Russian commissars on sight, in violation of the rules of war. Their objections brought a response from Keitel that was to count against him at Nuremberg, implicating him in atrocities which brought shame on the Wehrmacht.

'These anxieties belong to the concept of chivalrous warfare. Here we are engaged in the destruction of an ideology. For this reason I approve of the measures and stand by them.'

He also signed the infamous Decree on the Exercise of Military Jurisdiction, which declared, 'For acts committed by members of the Wehrmacht against enemy civilians, there is no obligation to prosecute, even when the act constitutes a military crime or offence.'

Those who knew him as Nickesel (the 'nodding donkey') and Hitler's 'Yes Man', refused to believe Keitel's assertion that he had 'the sharpest and harshest clashes with Hitler'. Nor could they swallow the notion that he had considered suicide rather than carry out the Führer's murderous orders.

Hitler and Mussolini pore over maps for the German propaganda sheet *Signal*, watched by Keitel (standing behind) and General Jodl

'Had I taken my life, I wouldn't have improved things, because this demon went ahead with whatever he wanted and succeeded... He was a demon-like man, possessed of inordinate willpower, who, whenever he had something in his mind, had to accomplish it.'

WILHELM KEITEL

BORN: 22 September, 1882, Helmscherode, Brunswick, German Empire
DIED: 16 October, 1946, Nuremberg, Germany
NICKNAME: *Lakeitel, Nickesel, Yes Man*

Family: Father: Carl Keitel, landowner; mother: Apollonia (née Vissering); wife: Lisa (née Fontaine); children: Karl-Heinz, Hans-Georg, Ernst-Wilhelm and three others (one of whom died in infancy)

Career/life: Joined army in 1908; fought with distinction in First World War; remained in Reichswehr after war, and rose to major-general by 1935, as head of Armed Forces Office; became full general and German war minister, 1937; promoted to field marshal in 1940; foiled July plot against Hitler, 1944; member of Flensburg government after Hitler's suicide; signed unconditional surrender, Berlin 1945; tried at Nuremberg for war crimes, having signed dozens of illegal orders and executed by hanging

Description: Educated, had the bearing of a senior officer, competent soldier and administrator; ascetic, upstanding in personal life (renounced limousine for VW because of a fuel crisis when war minister), but weakly condoned all of Hitler's war crimes as a matter of 'duty' to a superior, signing many orders that broke the conventions of warfare

'Hitler wanted a weak general in that powerful position in order to be able to have complete control of him.' **Ewald von Kleist**

THE FRITSCH SCANDAL

In January 1938 Keitel was promoted Chief of Staff of OKW, the Armed Forces High Command, after his predecessor, General Fritsch, had been falsely accused of committing homosexual acts in a public place. The conspiracy to blackmail the general had been cooked up by Himmler and Goering, who hoped to succeed Fritsch. It was only after the general had been exonerated by an army court, and the one eyewitness exposed as a known criminal, that it was discovered there had been a case of mistaken identity. The real blackmail victim was a cavalry officer with a similar-sounding surname, Frisch. But by then the general's reputation had been irreparably damaged. The affair threatened to see the overthrow of the Nazi dictatorship by the outraged generals, but fortunately for Hitler the successful annexation of Austria followed shortly afterwards, appeasing their anger.

WHAT WAR CRIMES?

Hitler himself complained that Keitel had the brain of a 'cinema usher' and that he had only appointed him Chief of Staff because he was the ideal 'office manager'.

After signing the surrender of the German armed forces in May 1945, Keitel was taken to Nuremberg to await trial for war crimes. Though stripped of his insignia and his medals his jailers soon had the measure of him. They joked that he would have made a fine first sergeant, meaning that he was a smug arrogant exhibitionist, incapable of leadership but suited to repetitive drilling and discipline.

The prison psychologist, Leon Goldensohn, found Keitel ingratiating, insincere and highly indignant that he, a military officer of the old school, should be accused of war crimes.

> 'I was field marshal in name only. I had no troops, no authority – only to carry out Hitler's orders. I was bound to him by oath. One of Hitler's prime ideas was that each minister and functionary was to mind his own business. That's why I learned about some of the [war-crime] business for the first time in this court.'

Keitel can be seen in the third row, almost directly behind Hitler, at Nuremberg, 1936, which indicates his status within the Party

The leaders of the three forces sign the German surrender: Stumpff (Luftwaffe), Keitel (Wehrmacht) and Von Friedeburg (Kriegsmarine)

WILHELM KEITEL DOSSIER

› Keitel enlisted in the army only because his father refused to allow him to manage the family estates.

› He saw action in the First World War at the battles of Verdun and Passchendaele, for which he was awarded the Iron Cross Ist and 2nd class.

› He was present in the Wolf's Lair, Hitler's East Prussian headquarters, on 20 July 1944 when the assassination attempt on Hitler's life took place. He was the only senior officer to escape the bomb blast uninjured.

› Keitel's brother, General Bodewin Keitel, intercepted a telegram from the July plotters at his command post in Danzig and prevented the coup from gathering momentum.

› The Keitel family purchased their father's ashes from the US Army after he was executed at Nuremberg and scattered them on the graves of his brother Bodewin and youngest son Hans-Georg, who had been killed in action in 1941.

Alfred Rosenberg

The Nazis' Self-styled Philosopher

'I didn't say that the Jews are inferior. I didn't even maintain they are a race. I merely saw that the mixture of different cultures didn't work.'

PERSECUTION MANIA

Alfred Rosenberg instructed Nuremberg prison psychiatrist Leon Goldensohn to make accurate notes so as not to misrepresent his 'rather complex theories and reasoning', which Goldensohn interpreted as an indication of the Nazi 'philosopher's' arrogance and his assumption that everyone was his intellectual inferior. In contrast, Goldensohn concluded that Rosenberg possessed a second-rate mind and was a man who mistook pomposity for profundity. He diagnosed Rosenberg as suffering from acute envy, bitterness and a persecution mania. He had slavishly recorded every minor compliment he thought Hitler had bestowed on him, but like a petulant child he was deeply wounded by every perceived slight.

> *'In the evenings the Führer often used to invite this man or that for a long fireside discussion. Apart from the usual guests at his table, Goebbels, Ley and some others were favoured in this respect. I can say nothing on this subject as I was not once invited.'*

DESPISED BY HIS COLLEAGUES

When Major Airey Neave entered his cell at Nuremberg to serve the indictment he found Rosenberg a dejected and pathetic figure, whose appearance was somewhere between 'an off-duty undertaker and a sick spaniel'. By the end of the trial Neave had heard enough to conclude, 'He had the greatest capacity for making the simplest proposition complicated and obscure.'

Hitler, too, had the measure of him. After he was sentenced to four years in prison for leading the Munich Putsch in 1924, Hitler appointed Rosenberg temporary head of the Nazi Party, not because Rosenberg possessed leadership qualities but because he lacked them. Hitler reasoned that if he appointed a strong personality he might lose the leadership by the time he was released from prison. Rosenberg was naturally honoured by the appointment and became an even more devoted servant, but he would have been aware that Hitler's closest aides, particularly Goering and Goebbels, despised him. They recognized a hypocrite when they saw one. Rosenberg was the only virulent anti-Semite in the Nazi hierarchy who made no secret of having a Jewish mistress.

When Hitler assumed power as Chancellor in January 1933, he continued to lavish pretentious titles on the Party's self-proclaimed 'philosopher', none of which carried real power, as if enjoying a perverse private joke. He would compliment Rosenberg on having written an 'intelligent book', but in private he told his inner circle that *The Myth of the Twentieth Century* was 'derivative' and 'illogical rubbish'. Goebbels agreed, condemning it as an 'ideological belch' and nicknaming Rosenberg 'Almost' because he 'almost managed to become a scholar, a journalist, a politician, but only almost'.

RACIST THEORIES

Rosenberg was the son of a wealthy Estonian merchant and looked set for a career as an architect or engineer until the Russian Revolution forced him to flee to Germany in 1918. A year later he joined the German

Workers' Party after reading Houston Stewart Chamberlain's irrational racist tract *The Foundations of the Nineteenth Century*, which fed his fanatical hatred for the Bolsheviks, whom he saw as the manifestation of a worldwide Jewish conspiracy. He then became the editor of the Party's newspaper, the *Völkischer Beobachter*, which gave him the platform to discharge his bizarre and illogical racist theories promoting the myth of the Aryan 'master race' and the inferiority of the Slavs, Jews and Gypsies. Rosenberg was also violently homophobic, which didn't win him any friends in the SA but ensured that he was a seminal influence on Nazi ideology.

But he always remained an outsider because of his Estonian origins and he was rarely taken seriously by those who knew him well. This made him all the more desperate for acceptance in his adopted country. Consequently, his racist theories became increasingly fanciful and irrational, while he grew intolerant of other people's opinions.

A Party colleague observed,

> *'In conversation one had the impression that he was not listening properly at all. Every now and then he would purse his lips when critical remarks were made or attempt a supercilious smile, which naturally gained him the reputation of arrogant unamiability... he had entirely lost his [...] underdeveloped capacity for making contact and entering into conversation with other people.'*

Journalist Max Amann was less diplomatic, describing his former editor as 'a buffoon'.

FINAL HUMILIATION

By late 1944, Rosenberg had finally come to the realization that he had lost his Führer's attention and that his memos and reports were being gleefully ignored by other departments. It was a crushing blow to his ego and prestige, made all the more damning when he learned that his best-selling book may have been widely distributed but remained largely unread. He was not the respected figure he had imagined himself to be. The final humiliation came when he tendered his resignation from his ministerial post only to have it disregarded. There was no impassioned plea for him to remain, no acknowledgement of his faithful service. Evidently, no one cared whether he remained or resigned.

Perhaps that is why, when he was asked if he had any last words before he died, he simply replied 'No.'

ALFRED ROSENBERG

BORN: 12 January, 1893, Reval (now Tallinn), Estonia
DIED: 16 October, 1946, Nuremberg, Germany
NICKNAME: 'Almost Rosenberg'

Family: Father: Waldemar Rosenberg, wealthy merchant; mother: Elfriede (née Siré); wives: Hilda, Hedwig; children (by Hedwig): Irene and son who died in infancy

Career/life: Joined German Workers' Party in 1919; member of Thule Society; editor of *Völkischer Beobachter*, 1923; puppet Nazi leader, 1923; anti-Semitic book on racial theory, 1930; chief Nazi racial theorist, propounded 'master race' theory, 1934, decried Christianity; in charge of occupied Eastern territories, 1941; tried and executed at Nuremberg, 1946

Description: Seen as cold and arrogant by colleagues, someone who saw others as his intellectual inferiors

'Anti-Semitism is the unifying element of the reconstruction of Germany.'

OVERLEAF: The Old Guard of the Hitler movement in 1923. Rosenberg is third from left in the middle row. Hitler's dog is in the front row

Julius Streicher

The Man Who Educated the German People in Hatred

'The charge that I have something to do with having stirred up the populace by propaganda or by my speeches to commit such atrocities is false... My conscience is as clear as a baby's.'

Julius Streicher – editor and publisher of the rabidly anti-Semitic journal *Der Stürmer* – was described as 'one of the two genuine nutcases' by a US Army psychologist and by US Army intelligence officer Lieutenant Dolibois as one of the 'real Nazi trash', a group which also included Dr Robert Ley, the Labour Minister, and Hans Frank, the 'Butcher of Poland'.

SEXUAL SADIST

Leon Goldensohn, a Jewish US Army psychiatrist who interviewed all of the Nuremberg defendants repeatedly over a course of six months, was prepared to study Streicher face to face and remained admirably frank in his appraisal.

> '*Streicher is a short, almost bald, hook-nosed figure of sixty-one years... He smiles constantly, the smile something between a grimace and a leer, twisting his large, thin-lipped mouth, screwing up his froggy eyes, a caricature of a lecher posing as a man of wisdom... He seems to me to be a man of probably limited normal intelligence, generally ignorant, obsessed with maniacal anti-Semitism, which serves as an outlet for his sexual conflicts, as evidenced by his preoccupation with pornography. Circumcision is a diabolical Jewish plot, and a clever one, he said, to preserve the purity of the Jewish stock. Christ, a Jew, was born of a mother who was a Jewish whore... (But) he denies any personal animosity toward the Jews.*'

Dr Goldensohn concluded that Streicher was a sexual sadist whose pathological obsession with Jews and the lurid acts he imagined they perpetrated upon innocent Aryan girls was most likely a projection of his own inner conflicts, inadequacy and perverse impulses.

Streicher had been jailed at Nuremberg many years before on charges of indecency after assaulting a young boy with a bullwhip and boasting that it had given him sexual gratification. Now, as he awaited the verdict of the Allied judges, he taunted his guards with details of his lurid dreams and offered to show them physical evidence of his sexual potency.

Old school and new breed: General von Schobert with Streicher

UNPOPULAR

When he was served with the indictment by Major Airey Neave, a British judicial aide who had made a daring escape from Colditz, Streicher was pacing his cell 'like an ape exposing himself in a cage' with his shirt open and his hands on his hips in a gesture of defiance. He struck Major Neave as 'stupid, cunning and cruel', someone who would have made an Inquisitor. 'I am without friends,' he told the major, who didn't express any surprise.

The other defendants objected to sitting in the same dock as the 'obscene dwarf' and 'degenerate', who was known to possess the largest private collection of pornography in Germany. Goering was particularly eager to distance himself from Streicher, who had published slanderous lies about his family and hoarded stolen property from deported Jews that Goering had once had his eye on. Stealing from the Reichsmarschall was considered a cardinal sin.

STRIPPED OF HIS TITLES

As a reward for playing a central role in the Munich Putsch, Streicher was given the post of Gauleiter of Franconia, where his home city, Nuremberg, was located. At first token appointees, Gauleiters acquired enormous authority when the Nazis came to power in 1933, which Streicher used to tighten his grip on Nuremberg. In particular, he ordered a one-day boycott of Jewish businesses. All of this was taken away from him in 1940, when his feud with Goering and aggressive use of his Gauleiter post resulted in his being stripped of his Party functions. He was allowed to go on publishing *Der Stürmer*, however. If it had not been for Hitler's enthusiastic support for *Der Stürmer*, its publisher would have been seen to have been an embarrassment to the educated Nazis long before that time.

> '*My publication was for a fine purpose. Certain snobs may now look down on it and call it common or even pornographic, but until the end of the war I had Hitler's greatest respect, and* Der Stürmer *had the Party's complete support. At our height we had a circulation of 1.5 million. Everybody read* Der Stürmer, *and they must have liked it or they wouldn't have bought it. The aim of* Der Stürmer *was to unite Germans and to awaken them against Jewish influence which might ruin our noble culture.*'

JULIUS STREICHER

BORN: 12 February, 1885, Fleinhausen, Bavaria
DIED: 16 October, 1946, Nuremberg, Germany
NICKNAME: Beast of Franconia, Jew-baiter Number One

Family: Father: Friedrich Streicher, teacher; mother: Anna (née Weiss); one of nine children; wife: Kunigunde (née Roth); children: Lothar, Elmar

Career/life: Joined German Army in 1914, decorated and commissioned; active in anti-Semitic organization, 1919, then led branch of German Socialist Party, 1920; merged with Nazi Party, 1922, and founded *Der Stürmer* 1923; part of Munich Putsch, then appointed Gauleiter of Franconia, 1925, where he exceeded his authority on many occasions; alienated Nazi Party and was stripped of offices, 1940; hanged at Nuremberg, 1946, though hanging was botched and prolonged

Description: Short, bald, hook-nosed, malevolent expression, degenerate, disliked by almost everyone

'The Jew is a devil in human form. It is fitting that he be exterminated root and branch.'

SENTENCED FOR HIS PRE-WAR ACTIVITIES

But if he thought that his lack of participation in the war might earn him a lighter sentence, he was rudely mistaken. His years of inciting racial hatred had put paid to that.

'Since 1940, I lived as a gentleman farmer in Furth. Hitler must have decided to exterminate the Jews in 1941, because I knew nothing about it. Hitler probably felt that "they caused the war, now I will exterminate them". I think that it was the wrong policy.'

Despite his vehement protestations of innocence the judges at Nuremberg found him guilty and sentenced him to death.

'For twenty-five years he educated the German people in the philosophy of hate, of brutality, of murder,' argued the British prosecution. 'He incited and prepared them to support the Nazi policy, to accept and participate in the brutal persecution and slaughter of his fellow men. Without him, these things could not have been. He forfeited any right to live a long time ago.'

Streicher clumsily follows Hitler and his enemy Goering in raising his right hand in the Luitpold hall at the 1937 Nuremberg rally

TIMELINE

1889

APRIL 20 1889
Adolf Hitler born near Linz, Austria.

NOV 11 1918
First World War ends. Germany defeated.

JUNE 28 1919
Signing of the Versailles Treaty.

JULY 29 1921
Adolf Hitler elected leader of National Socialist German Workers' Party.

NOV 9 1923
The Munich Beer Hall Putsch fails. Hitler imprisoned.

JULY 18 1925
Mein Kampf published.

OCT 29 1929
Wall Street stock market crash ushers in the Great Depression. Results in widespread inflation and high unemployment in America and Europe.

SEPT 14 1930
Nazis second-largest political party in Germany.

JAN 30 1933
Adolf Hitler becomes Chancellor of Germany.

MARCH 24 1933
As a result of the Reichstag fire of 27 Feb, Hitler invokes emergency powers.

APRIL 1 1933
Nazis encourage boycott of Jewish businesses.

MAY 10 1933
Ritual book-burning in German cities.

JULY 14 1933
Nazis outlaw opposition parties.

JUNE 30 1934
'The Night of the Long Knives'

JULY 25 1934
Nazis murder Austrian Chancellor Dollfuss.

AUG 2 1934
Death of German President von Hindenburg.

AUG 19 1934
Adolf Hitler is confirmed as Führer.

SEPT 15 1935
Nuremberg Race Laws deny Jews equal rights.

MARCH 7 1936
German troops occupy the Rhineland unopposed.

JULY 18 1936
Civil war in Spain. Fascists under Franco receive military aid from Germany.

AUG 1 1936
Olympic Games open in Berlin.

JUNE 11 1937
Soviet Army severely weakened and demoralized after Stalin instigates purge of senior Red Army officers.

MARCH 12 1938
Germany's Anschluss (union) with Austria.

SEPT 30 1938
British Prime Minister Neville Chamberlain signs Munich Agreement guaranteeing Britain and her Allies will not intervene if Hitler 'reclaims' the Sudetenland. Chamberlain claims he has secured 'peace in our time' by appeasing Hitler and preventing a European war.

OCT 15 1938
German troops occupy the Sudetenland.

NOV 9 1938
Kristallnacht (The Night of Broken Glass). Throughout Germany, Nazi thugs and their supporters smash the windows of Jewish businesses and set synagogues on fire.

1938

TIMELINE

1939

MARCH 15–16 1939
Nazis take Czechoslovakia.

MARCH 28 1939
Spanish Civil War ends.
Franco's fascists take power.

MAY 22 1939
Nazis sign 'Pact of Steel' with Italy.

AUG 21 1939
Nazis and Soviets sign Non-aggression Pact,
leaving Germany free to attack the West without
fear of a second front being opened up to the east.

AUG 25 1939
In response Britain and Poland
sign a Mutual Assistance Treaty.

SEPT 1 1939
Nazis invade Poland.

SEPT 3 1939
Britain, France, Australia and
New Zealand declare war on Germany.

SEPT 17 1939
Soviet Army invades Poland.
Ten days later, Poland surrenders.

SEPT 29 1939
Nazis and Soviets divide up Poland.

OCTOBER 1939
Nazis instigate euthanasia policy.
The sick and disabled are exterminated.

NOV 8 1939
Assassination attempt on Hitler fails.

NOV 30 1939
Soviet Army invades Finland. On 12 March,
Finland signs a peace treaty.

APRIL 9 1940
Nazis invade Denmark and Norway.

MAY 10 1940
Blitzkrieg! Nazis invade France, Belgium,
Luxembourg and the Netherlands.
Winston Churchill appointed British Prime Minister.

MAY 15 1940
Holland surrenders.
Belgium capitulates on May 28.

MAY 26 1940
Evacuation of Allied troops from Dunkirk.
Ends June 3.

JUNE 10 1940
Norway surrenders; Italy declares war
on Britain and France.

JUNE 14 1940
German troops enter Paris.

JUNE 16 1940
Marshal Pétain becomes French Prime Minister.

JUNE 18 1940
Hitler and Mussolini form alliance;
Soviets occupy the Baltic States.

JUNE 22 1940
Hitler humiliates France by forcing its leaders to sign
an armistice in the same railway carriage in which
Germany signed the surrender in 1918.

JUNE 28 1940
Britain recognizes the exiled General Charles
de Gaulle as the leader of the Free French.
In France the 'puppet' Vichy government
collaborates with the Nazis.

JULY 1 1940
German U-boat campaign begins in the
Atlantic harassing merchant convoys
bringing vital supplies to the British Isles.

JULY 10 1940
Battle of Britain begins. Throughout August,
German bombers target British airfields and
factories. The British respond by bombing Berlin –
the first long-range raid of the war.

SEPT 13 1940
Italians invade Egypt.

SEPT 15 1940
German air raids extend to Southampton,
Bristol, Cardiff, Liverpool and Manchester.

SEPT 27 1940
Axis formed when Germany, Italy and
Japan sign the Tripartite Pact.

OCT 7 1940
German troops invade Romania.

OCT 12 1940
Germans cancel Operation Sealion.

OCT 28 1940
Italian Army invades Greece.

NOV 20 1940
Hungary joins the Axis followed
three days later by Romania.

DEC 9–10 1940
British North African campaign
begins against the Italians.

1940

TIMELINE

1941

JAN 22 1941
British and Australians take strategically vital North African port of Tobruk which will change hands several times after Rommel's Afrika Korps enter the desert theatre on 12 Feb.

MAY 10 1941
Deputy Führer Rudolf Hess flies to Scotland and is arrested.

JUNE 1941
Nazi SS Einsatzgruppen begin programme of mass murder in Latvia.

JULY 3 1941
Stalin orders a scorched earth policy in the face of the advancing Germans.

JULY 31 1941
Goering instructs Heydrich to instigate the Final Solution – the mass extermination of the Jews in Germany.

SEPT 3 1941
First experimental use of gas chambers at Auschwitz.

DEC 7 1941
Japanese bomb Pearl Harbor.

DEC 19 1941
Hitler takes complete command of the German Army.

MAY 30 1942
First thousand-bomber British air raid (against Cologne).

JUNE 4 1942
Heydrich dies after assassination attempt in Prague. Nazis liquidate Lidice in reprisal.

JULY 1–30 1942
First Battle of El Alamein.

JAN 14–24 1943
At Casablanca, Churchill and Roosevelt demand the unconditional surrender of Germany.

FEB 2 1943
Encircled Germans surrender at Stalingrad.

APRIL 19 1943
Waffen SS launch assault on Jewish resistance group in the Warsaw ghetto. Resistance holds out until 16 May.

JULY 9–10 1943
Allies land in Sicily.

OCT 1 1943
Allies enter Naples, Italy.

MARCH 27 1941
A coup in Yugoslavia overthrows the pro-Axis government.

APRIL 6 1941
Nazis invade Greece and Yugoslavia. The latter surrenders on 17 April. Greece surrenders ten days later.

MAY 27 1941
Nazi flagship, the *Bismarck*, sunk by the British Navy.

JUNE 22 1941
German invasion of Soviet Union codenamed Operation Barbarossa.

JULY 12 1941
British and Soviets sign Mutual Assistance Agreement.

SEPT 1 1941
Nazis order Jews to wear yellow stars.

OCT 2 1941
Operation Typhoon begins (German advance on Moscow). Withdrawal begins 5 Dec. Four days later, Soviet Army launches a major counter-offensive around Moscow. German retreat begins.

JAN 20 1942
SS Leader Heydrich holds the Wannsee Conference to co-ordinate the 'Final Solution'.

JUNE 1942
Mass murder of Jews begins at Auschwitz.

JUNE 11 1942
Himmler orders the destruction of Jewish ghettos in Poland.

SEPT 1942
Battle of Stalingrad begins.

JAN 27 1943
First American bombing raid on Germany.

FEB 18 1943
Nazis arrest White Rose resistance leaders in Munich.

MAY 13 1943
German and Italian troops surrender in North Africa.

JULY 25–26 1943
Mussolini arrested and replaced by Marshal Badoglio. He is rescued six weeks later by the Germans.

1943

TIMELINE

1944

JAN 22 1944
Allies land at Anzio.

FEB 15–18 1944
Allies bomb the monastery of Monte Cassino.

JUNE 5 1944
Allies enter Rome.

JUNE 6 1944
D-Day landings.

JUNE 22 1944
The Soviet summer offensive begins the rout of the German invaders.

JULY 20 1944
Hitler survives assassination attempt at the 'Wolf's Lair' HQ.

AUG 25 1944
Paris liberated.

SEPT 17 1944
Operation Market Garden begins (Allied airborne assault on Holland).

OCT 14 1944
Allies liberate Athens; Rommel commits suicide on Hitler's orders for his part in the July plot.

DEC 26 1944
The 'Battling Bastards of Bastogne' relieved by General Patton. The Germans withdraw from the Ardennes during January. Hitler's last gamble has failed.

FEB 13–14 1945
Dresden is destroyed by a firestorm after Allied bombing raids.

APRIL 1 1945
US troops encircle remnants of German Army in the Ruhr. They surrender on 18 April.

APRIL 16 1945
Americans enter Nuremberg.

APRIL 21 1945
Soviets enter Berlin.

APRIL 29 1945
US 7th Army liberates Dachau.

MAY 7 1945
The unconditional surrender of the German forces is signed.

MAY 9 1945
Hermann Goering surrenders to US 7th Army.

JUNE 5 1945
Allies partition Germany and divide Berlin into sections. The Cold War begins.

JAN 27 1944
The siege of Leningrad is lifted after 900 days.

MARCH 4 1944
First major daylight bombing raid on Berlin by the Allies.

JUNE 13 1944
First German V1 rocket attack on Britain.

JULY 3 1944
'Battle of the Hedgerows' in Normandy. A week later, Caen is liberated.

JULY 24 1944
Soviet troops liberate first concentration camp at Majdanek.

SEPT 13 1944
US troops reach the Siegfried Line.

OCT 2 1944
Polish Home Army forced to surrender to the Germans in Warsaw after weeks of heroic resistance.

DEC 16–27 1944
Battle of the Bulge in the Ardennes. Retreating Waffen SS murder 81 US POWs at Malmedy.

JAN 26 1945
Soviet troops liberate Auschwitz.

FEB 4–11 1945
Roosevelt, Churchill, Stalin meet at Yalta and plan the partition of post-war Germany.

APRIL 1945
Allies recover stolen Nazi art hidden in salt mines.

APRIL 12 1945
Allies uncover the horrors of the 'Final Solution' at Buchenwald and Belsen concentration camps; President Roosevelt dies. Truman becomes President.

APRIL 28 1945
Mussolini is hanged by Italian partisans.

APRIL 30 1945
Adolf Hitler commits suicide in the Berlin bunker, followed by the suicide of Goebbels. The corpses are burnt.

MAY 8 1945
VE (Victory in Europe) Day.

MAY 23 1945
SS Reichsführer Himmler commits suicide.

NOV 20 1945
Nuremberg war crimes trials begin. Goering will commit suicide almost a year later, two hours before his scheduled execution.

1945

INDEX

INDEX

A soldier hoists the Soviet flag over the
Reichstag after the fall of Berlin in 1945.

PICTURE CREDITS

Below
Hitler and Goebbels salute a Nazi future during the Reich convention of the NSDAP